The Odyssey of a War Orphan

"The test of one's mettle is how he or she faces conflict"

A Memoir

Maria A. Beurmann

Dedication

To Lisa and to her progeny - my
"favorite" grandchildren, Michael and Rachel -
in whom I see my hopes and dreams.

And to my mother, Bertha Russo,
a woman who allowed me to truly endure.

Acknowledgements

Special thanks to...   David Martin, Megan Peyron and
Grace Thedinga for their attention to detail and their
assurances that this work of non-fiction follows reality in its
language, grammar and meaning.

"All the mistakes you see are mine."

An Obsession

To think in images,
A fantasy world of words
That weaves a complex tapestry.

A mind full of ideas and experiences
That forcefully rise to the top of awareness
To embellish a blank page.

A flourish of terms
To convey a smell, a sight, an emotion,
To ensure that the event is *not* only one's own.

- Maria A. Beurmann

Prologue

It was Thanksgiving. My encounter group was relishing the food, the company of new friends and the spirit of togetherness. We were a mixed bag of professions and backgrounds – a lawyer, two teachers, an architect and an Assistant to the Attorney General of Vermont and my daughter, Julia, but most of us were in search for the light at the end of the tunnel. We had experienced divorce or a loss of a loved one and this feast marked a new beginning.

I was intent on eating and was half-listening to my tablemate's conversation. He may have wanted to entertain the group as he turned toward me and speared a piece of food from my plate. Without a thought, I pierced his hand with my fork. His screams stopped the holiday activities as he was rushed to the nearest hospital.

My friend's innocent attempt at humor resurrected memories of starvation, poverty and the suffering I experienced as a child in Italy in the final years of World War II.

Chapter 1

"Mi chiama Marietta Fatichenti"

Rough, wooden-slated walls allowed a view of the countryside in the throes of war. The four year old Marietta and her younger brother sat on a plank bed waiting for their mother. They were hungry, but there was little food to be found in Montepulciano, Italy. At times, the soldiers who frequented the area shared their rations with the two starving children, but it was never enough. When a chocolate bar was offered by an American soldier the children clutched it like a gift from heaven.

Their father was long gone. He might have decided to continue living in the area or he might have absconded to a wealthier province, but the children no longer saw him since he left the responsibility of raising the girl and boy to the mother. Because of the lack of food and clothing the mother was forced to foster her children in separate orphanages. My brother was housed in a boy's only orphanage while I was placed in a girl's Catholic orphanage in Rome, Italy. With the move, my brother was forever lost to me and I never returned to my birthplace, Montepulciano.

World War II affected every aspect of Italy's life and my orphanage was not exempt. Our main meals were usually spinach soup or boiled tripe. We had a scarcity of vegetables and fruit but, occasionally, my mother would bring oranges. These were immediately hoarded by the nuns who managed the orphanage. The temptation to steal the food that my mother had brought me was hard to resist. I remember crawling in the dark under the dining room tables hoping to take one of the oranges from the locked hutch. All I can recall of that adventure were the lights going on. Since the orphanage was managed by a pastor and the nuns and women from the city, I probably was punished. The rigors of war - violence and poverty - frustrated and frightened the denizens of the city, so beatings and abuse were common.

Hunger ruled our lives. As a little girl, I would scour with the other children the hard-packed dirt in the enclosed yard for scraps of bread. The citizens of the city would often feed the birds that gathered on the fence. We would also gather around a toilet to decide who was going to benefit from the harvest of feces. The search for food cost me the use of my right hand for a period of time. I was foraging the ground for scraps when a soldier accidentally crushed my hand with his boot. My hand still bears the stigma of that injury.

The orphans had adequate living quarters. The girls slept in one large room. A corner of the room was portioned off by a large white sheet for the nun who supervised the sleeping area. She had a regular bed to sleep on while the little girls slept on beds of straw. If sick, the child was given a hospital bed in the infirmary. I spent a year cloistered in the infirmary when I contracted Tuberculosis by drinking unpasteurized milk. I also had seasonal malnutrition diseases that were manifested as lesions about my ears and mouth. I was a sickly and weak child.

Since the orphanage was considered by many outsiders as a safe haven because it housed children, it was a constant target for enemy planes. My shrapnel wounds attest to the attacks on our sleeping quarters.

The numerous scars on my head were from our guardians. I can understand as an adult that the nuns and aides may have been irritated by the needs of frail, sick and terrified little girls. In my mind's eye, I can still recall the blood that streaked the tub. Because of my weakened state I could not open the water faucet to fill the tub for my weekly bath. The frustrated aide grabbed my head and thrust it through the pronged handles. She was immediately fired but I have always felt compelled as an adult to explain to new hairdressers, nurses and doctors why my head is a mass of ridges and indentations.

The four years as a ward of the orphanage run by the Catholic Charities passed in a blur. Holidays were the high point of the year for us. We were given the honor of playing the characters that were endemic to the seasonal feast. I played Christ and carried a wooden cross throughout the church on an Easter Sunday. During Christmas, we created a living tableau of Mary, Joseph, the shepherds and the wise men. A local baby was given the part of Jesus. These plays provided unique religious experiences for the abandoned girls.

Chapter 2

"Mi chiama Marietta Fatichenti"

My eighth birth year proved to be a pivotal year. An American teacher, Bertha Russo, contacted the pastor of the Sacred Heart Orphanage in Rome in 1951. He had in the past been an interim pastor in Fredonia, New York where the teacher lived. Bertha also knew the bishop of New York City and she was able to convince both clergymen to expedite an adoption. It was very unusual to have a single woman adopt a child in the 1950's.

My future mother had been convinced by her wealthy cousins that she needed a servant to help care for her mother and to help around the house; however, her cousins had an ulterior motive for pushing the adoption; they themselves wanted to use the child as a servant.

I was a poor choice. The pastor must have glorified my qualities, but as an adult I realized that my mother trusted too much and was too easily swayed by religion and authority.

The nuns were thrilled by my upcoming adoption. They filled my head with stories of money growing on trees and streets paved with gold. Truthfully, they were relieved to get rid of me. I was a mess; I was sickly, too old and was starting to develop a headstrong personality. My only future, if I were to remain in the orphanage, was to be sold to a local family where I *would* be a servant.

The Catholic Charities, through the bishop's influence, sponsored my plane ride to New York City. Much to my surprise, I did not see open wealth but was greeted by tall buildings, darkness, noise and rain. My adopted mother met me there. After a night's sleep, my new parent, a cousin and I traveled to Fredonia, New York.

Fredonia is a small college town that is known for its extensive grape vineyards, its ambiance, its farmlands, its heavy snows and its bars. Johnny Carson, a famous television personality, used the last fact as part of his opening repertoire during one of his late-night television shows.

There did seem to be more bars than people when I attended SUNY – Fredonia in the 1960's.

My mother shared her home in Fredonia with her mother. I was given the luxury of a room on the second floor which provided me with a view of the street and a busy elementary school.

After living in the midst of a war with other orphans and a staff as company for four years, I was lonely in my new home. I was anxious and tended to keep to myself, but I was well taken care of by my new parent. I was given food; plain but filling; however, the specter of hunger was ever present. My mother had to lock the door to the kitchen during the night hours to prevent me from emptying the refrigerator. When I visited the neighbors, I usually ate the entire contents of their sugar bowls. I even stole change and dollar bills that my grandmother had secreted in drawers to buy candy and to sate my sweet tooth at the local mom and pop store.

My favorite place to visit was my "Uncle Joe's" farm. He was my mother's cousin. I had the freedom to gorge myself on cherries, peaches and pears that grew on the trees that covered his farm. The summer days were idyllic. I would surfeit myself on fruit and ripe tomatoes and then play in the tall grasses, climb trees and explore the nearby creek.

I also looked forward to visiting Uncle Joe's house at midnight for a late dinner. Uncle Joe worked in a steel mill during the day. He was easing going, loved to laugh, played various musical instruments and was partial to children, so I felt accepted and part of his family. I consider him to be my foremost mentor, since I learned from his example to take risks, to be creative and to attempt activities that were not gender based. I would watch him fix furnaces, trim trees, train dogs and work on his tractor. He took the time to answer my questions, but he focused on his task and did the job well.

His wife, my "Aunt Louise", would cook a wealth of Italian food for us at midnight, such as spaghetti and meatballs, hot peppers stuffed with cheddar cheese, or fried potatoes with sweet peppers, onions and eggs. She would follow the dinner with servings of sweet Italian deserts. On occasions, when my uncle had the early evening off from work, he would take out his accordion and play Italian music. The neighborhood children, my cousins and I would cavort about the living room until we were exhausted and ready for bed. These were some of my happiest childhood memories.

Chapter 3

"My name is Maria Fatichenti"

My adopted mother was a pioneer in the Fredonia school district. She was the first Roman Catholic teacher, the first female president of the Teachers' Union and the first female principal of the middle school. She was a hard worker and a survivor who was forced to live a lifestyle that reflected the mores of that period. When hired, she was given a list of rules which she had to follow, for example, she could not date without the school district's permission. Female teachers took on written and verbal strait jackets when they were hired.

Bertha Russo was a very private person who gave rather than received. She was committed to teaching and to caring for her mother. She had several older and one younger friend, her cousin, who shared her love of learning, the arts, children and reading. She may not have been loved by many, but she was respected. When my adopted mother passed away, her wake was held in Fredonia, as it was her wish. She had been away from her home, and housed near me for 20 years because of illness, yet over 75 people attended the wake to pay their respects. She was highly regarded, and many credited her for their success.

Her mother and she had survived the Great Depression, so frugality ruled our household. My mother would tell me that during the Great Depression her wardrobe consisted of only two dresses, one that she wore to teach which she washed at night and the second dress was reserved for the next day.

There were two meals that I loathe to this day that my family inherited from the Great Depression period. I get nauseous when I think of boiled chicken feet or a supper of a soup bone covered with fatty tissue. Steak repels me to this day if it is not trimmed of its fat.

There were some meals; however, that solely consist of my comfort foods. Even as an adult, I still favor potatoes, onions and green peppers fried in olive oil. I also make baked spaghetti, white fish and fennel in a tomato sauce base to celebrate St. Joseph's feast day (the patron saint of Italians).

A major regret in my mother's life was that she never married or dated. She had five offers of marriage, but her commitment to her mother made her decide to care for her until she passed away. Her Catholic upbringing, an old-world mentality and her occupation forced her to stay single. I believe that my adoption made life extremely difficult for her. I had so many liabilities; I was often ill, had a high energy level and was stubborn, but she never gave up on me.

My mother had to contend with an elderly mother who was very conservative, was ultra - religious, and wore multiple layers of dark, floor-length clothes that smelled of age. My grandmother walked with a cane and was very aggressive toward me. She must have felt that I usurped her position with her daughter.

I did not initially have any friends. My grandmother was the person with whom I spent the most time. We spoke different dialects of the same language, but did not understand each other. We shared no personal experiences. We were literally worlds apart.

Since our backgrounds were so disparate, I found ways to amuse myself. I wandered the neighborhood and spent time with the women of the neighborhood. I would tell my grandmother tales to agitate her to the point where she would insist on visiting the neighbors to chastise them. My grandmother would rail at them in the Sicilian dialect while leaning on her cane, and I would goad her on in my Tuscan dialect. It must have been a free-for-all for the neighbors. There were also many occasions when my grandmother and I would have shouting matches. They would end with my grandmother chasing me around the dining room table trying to hit me with her cane. She was not amused by my numerous antics.

Another way I would vent my youthful spirit was to swing on the dining room door. I would grab on to the top of the door with both hands, and would brace my feet on the door knobs and then would push off from the wall. The door would swing shut, but my body prevented it from closing. Like a monkey, I would push off again so that I could crash into the wall.

Unfortunately, after repeating my gymnastics again and again the door hinges gave out and the door and I crashed to the floor.

I had watched my Uncle Joe fix broken things, so I picked up the door and fit the screws into the original holes on the door jamb. I then propped the door against the wall and hoped that my mother would not notice the damage I had wrought.

When I was first adopted, my mother locked the same door to prevent me from eating her out of house and home, but now the door between the dining room and the kitchen was rarely closed.

I never swung on a door again. To this day, I don't know if my mother ever noticed what I had done to the door, but she may have just called my uncle to fix it.

Chapter 4

"My name is Maria Fatichenti"

When I was not seeking adventures in the great outdoors, I would sit in a little rocking chair in my bedroom and watch the world go by. That little chair now sits in my adult daughter's bedroom.

Since I was bedridden with pneumonia on many occasions, because of my having had Tuberculosis, I would read voraciously. My mother would bring a bag of books home each week from the library. I would devour science fiction, adventure, Marvel comics, fantasy, mystery, such as Nancy Drew, works by Sir Arthur Conan Doyle, Nero Wolfe and my favorite; mythology. Thor, Odin, Superman, Wonder

Woman, Hera and Hermes were my constant companions.

To this day, I still revel in stories of King Arthur and Avalon.

An Ancient Dirge

A mighty warrior is dead.

Let nubile virgins accompany him
Down a gilded path
To the moon-drenched river.

Lift the torches high
To illuminate his bearers,
His costly raiment of scarlet and black.
Let the flames flash
On golden crown and jewels
That grace his body.

Be quick to light the tapers
That line his barge.
Gently place him on a palette of thick furs.
Cover him with the fragrance of flowers.
Surround him with
Gem-encrusted sword and shield;
Companions that he wielded in battle.

Fear not the night wind.
It will carry him to
The Elysian Fields where
Gods and heroes will honor him.

Cry a dirge…

Sing a paean…
So he may begin his watery voyage.

A beloved hero is dead.

When these heroes were not enough, I would climb a chair and press my fingers on a crucifix that hung on the wall and be comforted with something familiar. At one time I entertained the idea of becoming a nun, but once I was able to bike about the town and countryside I discarded that ambition.

I may have been nine or ten when I had my first encounter with a neighbor who would be considered by today's standards a pedophile. This was my first introduction to anything remotely sexual. An eighty year old neighbor invited me into his home to touch and view his penis. I had never seen a man's privates before so in innocence I took the quarter that he offered to keep me silent. Because money was rare, I showed the quarter to another neighbor. That neighbor informed my mother of the man's indiscretion and all hell broke loose. The man's daughter met with me and apologized for her father's behavior. In retrospect, because of my lack of experience, no harm was done to me, but the neighborhood had a difficult time forgetting the event.

Chapter 5

"My name is Maria Fatichenti"

I was becoming acclimated to the neighborhood, was baseline efficient with the English language and began to branch out for new experiences. My grandmother could not keep up with my energy level and my mother was at her wit's end to find things for me to do when I was not in school.

I was an oddity in St. Joseph's Catholic Middle School since I was the only student who could not speak English well. I don't remember specific insults but I was bullied. I was chased up telephone poles, was pursued about the school grounds, and when I inherited a bike it was often stolen or knocked about.

On one occasion, I was nearly killed by a car as I was crossing a busy road to avoid being punched by a boy. We both received a dressing down by the head nun. She kept her eighth grade students focused in class by pulling their hair or by liberally applying the ruler to various body parts. I was one of her favorite recipients of this time-tested practice.

The bullying became extreme, so I retaliated by smashing my umbrella over my tormentor's head. It took a couple of years for the other students in my class to understand that I didn't appreciate their special attentions. I ruined over 10 umbrellas before the attacks stopped.

Ironically, when I was a freshman in college and working at Hunter's, I met a college student whom I had hit with an umbrella. Since I was starting to date and was attracted to his blue eyes, I was mortified by his recollection.

I also acquired another response to the attacks. When chased I would stop, grab the offending attacker and attempt to smash his head on the sidewalk. Surprisingly, there were no reprisals from the parents, but the boys may have been embarrassed to have been bested by a girl, or my mother might have interceded. I'll never know what came out of my survival skills.

Much to my mother's chagrin, I also became interested in flowers. During a lush spring, I passed a garden every morning that was filled with tulips and daffodils. I thought they were lovely and believed that they might be the ticket for changing the nun's attitude toward me. I brought a handful every day to school until the irate owner of the garden followed me and berated the nuns. I don't know if any restitution was made by my mother, but my practice of helping myself to something beautiful was short-lived. I may be giving myself too much credit, but I believe I was the bane of the nuns who ran the Catholic school. I know I was a handful for my mother.

Chapter 6

"My name is Maria Fatichenti"

My bike became my gateway to freedom. One of my favorite aunts gave me the bike because she probably had noticed that I had little to entertain myself with at home except to make little rag dolls. They were my companions and friends.

I became quite creative with them. The dolls' bodies were constructed with a   cloth core that had appendages (arms and legs) sewed to it. The dolls were only five inches long and each had an entire wardrobe made out of different colored cloth. Each also had different colored, long hair made of string. I could dress them and comb their hair at will. The dolls would sit on my mother's childhood, miniature set of wooden furniture to play out their imaginary lives. They even had a piano to practice on, but the furniture was so old and fragile that it soon had to be put aside.

When not in my bedroom creating worlds, I wandered for hours on my bike exploring streets and farmlands around Fredonia and Dunkirk, New York. I became part of a group of adventure-bound kids, mostly boys, who enjoyed swimming and playing in a local creek, who swung on ropes over cliffs and who climbed railroad trestles as the iron behemoth thundered overhead. We would hang on with white-knuckled death grips while the iron trestles rattled and shook as the screaming tonnage flew by.

I had some memorable adventures. On one occasion, I was swinging from a cliff over a chicken coup and lost my grip on the rope. I fell in the midst of the clucking chickens. Feathers and chickens flew everywhere, but by the time the owner came racing out of his house, I was long gone. I was bruised and shaken but not seriously hurt.

I was a tomboy. On winter mornings on my way to school I would grab a large branch, jump on an inflated tractor tire and push myself across a frozen pond. Surprisingly, I never broke through the ice. I also would sled down hills with the winter wind abrading my face, or would tunnel through legendary heights of snow banks. In retrospect, my life became much like one of my heroes, Huckleberry Finn.

At night, I would climb out of my second story window, shimmy down the pear tree and wander the streets basking in the solitude and an unbounded freedom.

A Constant

In my youth, unfettered and unformed,
I'd walk the streets of a small town,
To feel the wild, warm wind
That would tug and whip my hair and leaves,
And toss Great Lake waters into a froth.

A time of heat, innocence
And a gypsy questing
That drew others
Like moths to a flame.

An unclear need for solitude,
For budding life and a kindred soul
Drove my body to roam.

So many experiences and relationships later,
The quest is still strong.
Still a gypsy in spirit,
Only desiring the entangling, pulsating wind,
The open, starry skies
And the deep night to soothe the soul.

With autonomy, I gained more confidence and became more difficult to control at home. If I were especially problematic, my mother would force me to stand by her bedside while she slept. If I nodded off during the night she would wake me. I don't recall having this punishment often, but it was difficult as an adolescent to miss a night's sleep.

The worst punishment, which also worked but that I had difficulty forgiving her for, was that she deprived me of Christmas or Easter gifts and celebrations. I have a hazy recollection of the punishments that affected me the most as a ten or eleven year old. I just recall the darkness and misery of her lessons. As an adult, I made it a point to provide generous and happy holidays for my daughter and my grandchildren.

The most embarrassing "tough love" teachings my mother provided; however, were her calls to my Uncle Joe. I'm not certain why he constantly responded to my mother's requests to help her control my behavior, but up to the age of 15 he would appear at our doorstep and give me spankings for major infractions. It was common during the 50's to use a belt, a wooden spoon or a hand to keep a child in line.

When I turned 15 he sat me down at the kitchen table. He had just discovered me hiding high in a pear tree while the entire neighborhood was searching for me -the runaway child. He talked to me as if I were an adult. His advice to "Grow Up!" changed my behavior and became a major benchmark in my life.

Chapter 7

"My name is Maria Fatichenti"

Bertha never disclosed the reasons for her actions.
We did not have mother/daughter talks to discuss problems,
watch movies on the television together as the evening's
entertainment, or go for long walks, so there was a definite
lack of communication.

I relied on the radio for amusement, but while living
with my mother, the house was intensely quiet. It often
reminded me of the cathedral-like quiet of the church at the
orphanage. Thankfully, I could rely on my books for
entertainment.

By this time I had finished 8th grade, but I still did not
fully comprehend the English language, especially its idioms
or its subtleties. My mother did communicate with me in

English but she had to rely primarily on her knowledge of her mother's Italian dialect to get major ideas across.

My "language" in school was to fight and to run away. I was still painfully shy and, in my own neighborhood, would often hide behind trees. Then, I would not have to speak or have a conversation with an older child or an adult.

As a 9th grader, I was placed in a school run by The State University of New York (SUNY) at Fredonia. The Campus School was more progressive in its teachings and the students were not as prejudiced or as pugilistic as those at St. Joseph's. The students' parents were often professionals and not blue collar like those that attended the Catholic school.

I discovered that the students and professors were open-minded and much friendlier. I was befriended by both a biology teacher and a boy named Bob Hale. He made a point of inviting me to his church events that featured singing, conversation and food. He had many friends to whom he introduced me. He was very kind to a lonely teenager.

Because of his impact on me, I kept in contact with Bob through high school and college. I was able to repay his kindness as an adult, when I housed his Japanese wife and two children until they could fly to Thailand where he was stationed.

It was a sad situation. Bob's mom was badly affected by menopause. She became violent and struck out against her family. She refused to acknowledge Bob's wife and children. Tammi and her two girls were restricted to one room day and night and they were forced to walk to the grocery store to buy food. It was an extremely unpleasant time for both Tammi's father-in-law, who was unable to deal with his wife's manic behavior, and for Tammi, who wanted to be with her husband in Thailand, or with her family in Japan.

I also kept in contact with the biology professor who had taught me at the Campus school. I would visit him at the college or at his home when I traveled to Fredonia to visit my mother during holiday vacations or during the summer months.

The Campus school had a strong intellectual base and my biology professor became another mentor by igniting my interest in nature and biology. Ninth grade was a balm to my soul, for it was stimulating, I was making friends and I was happy.

By living in her household, my mother unconsciously instilled me with a strong work ethic. She got me jobs working on farms that hired teenagers to pick strawberries, grapes, currants and cherries. My reputation as a worker grew and my mother began to receive calls requesting my services. I did not yet possess the desire for clothes or makeup because I was ignorant of how important they were to other teens. The more I worked, the more I began to appreciate earning spending money for movies. Dean Martin and Jerry Lewis were some of my favorite actors.

I obtained summer and fall jobs because I was dexterous with my hands and was serious about the work. I still kept to myself even though I was surrounded by teenagers. My belief was that the other pickers, especially the girls, were prettier, smarter and when in school were better dressed. I was in awe of them.

After a couple of years of working for the same farmer, I was so proficient at picking fruit that I could pick the required number of crates each day and still have time to savor my first summer romance. Unfortunately for my employer, I was not a model worker for any teenagers starting a new job that summer. The kisses in the hot summer sun were a new and heady experience. They were intoxicating.

Recollections

As a woman-child, I danced in the moonlight
Among diminutive, vaporous fairies
And circles of capped mushrooms.

Full of energy and a need for the mysterious,
I clanged spoons as cymbals and waved towels as wings.
My bare feet imprinted dewed grass in silent, syncopated beats.

The sweet nectar of youth, a fresh love affair
And new friendships
Led me to abandon shyness, to spin like a firefly
In the silver rays of a full moon.

Chapter 8

"My name is Maria Fatichenti"

The aunts who had motivated my mother to adopt me also bullied her to have me work for them during the summer and on weekends while I attended the Campus School. They needed a gopher to work on their vast tracts of land, their vineyards, factory and in their apartment building which was and still is the largest building in Fredonia. They were wealthy, but extremely frugal.

The summer months that I worked in their factory I sorted strawberries. It was tedious work and often times not manageable. Hundreds of berries would fly by on a belt to be dumped into a large vat where they were washed and crushed. My job was to pick out the moldy fruit, but on several occasions a mouse would join spoiled fruit as they fell into the crusher. I could not eat strawberry jam for many years.

The most obnoxious jobs my relatives had me do were cleaning the rental apartments and the elevator. It was rank and filthy work.

My task was to scrub the walls and floor of the building's elevator every day I worked. College students would often creep into the Russo Building at night or during the day to vomit in the foyer and the elevator because of excessive drinking.

I had never been conscious of homeless people in the town but it seemed that every Tom, Dick and Harry was using the elevator as a toilet. As I became "Americanized" in the 1960's and found a regular job at Hunter's store, I told my mother "Basta" or "Enough." The cleaning jobs were revolting and demeaning, plus I don't remember ever being paid for the hours of work.

They also had me monitor the field hands in the Russo vineyards, but my job as a "manager" must have been seen as a joke by the migrant workers, especially since I was a young girl who could barely speak English. The workers must have really feared my three aunts because they treated me kindly when I would greet them. Thankfully, that summer passed quickly.

Since my relatives considered themselves above most families in the town because of their wealth and pedigree, my jobs did nothing to change their poor attitude toward my mother or me. My mother, as a school principal and a teacher, was still a church mouse in their eyes. It also irritated me that I never even received a "Thank you" for the work that I completed.

I shouldn't have been surprised when I got married as a junior in college and had my daughter, Julia, that they did not give me a wedding present. They did gift me with a packet of diapers for my daughter when she was born that still had the $1.98 price tag affixed to it. They later had the nerve to contact my mother and ask why I had not sent them a thank you note for the gift.

Chapter 9

"My name is Maria Fatichenti"

I was challenged during my enrollment at the Campus School with a problem that took me several years to resolve. It affected my mother and me, and forced me to transform myself.

My mother, as a traditional English teacher and as a principal, was often accused of wearing "army boots." She was tough and demanded excellence from her students. When she was diagnosed with Alzheimer's many years later, I would visit her in Fredonia and take her grocery shopping. We could not move down the aisle without having one of her former students stop us to regale me with an anecdote of my mother's teaching style. A recurring story was that she kept her students for hours after school to recite all the prepositions without any hesitations. Her reputation was well established when she adopted me, and as I sat in my bedroom gazing out of my window, I slowly became aware that there were some students who wanted revenge.

Unfortunately, my mother did not like her first name – Bertha. Since her mother had been born in Italy, my grandmother did not understand and speak English well. To make it easier for my mother to survive, my grandmother asked a close friend for the English translation of my mother's birth name – Fortunata. My grandmother's friend must not have been proficient in the English language because she stated that the Italian name, Fortunata, was Bertha when translated into English.

As kids normally tend to push the envelope, one of her students took the liberty of calling her Bertha while in class. My mother reacted forcefully to the disrespect and that began several years of name-calling.

As a youngster, I watched the elementary children leaving the school grounds with their parents, but I also would monitor the older students who were wending their way home. Invariably, they would glance toward my house and yell out "Bertha." Many of these students, I discovered, did not even have her as a teacher. They represented various ages and grades, because the practice was passed down to their younger sisters and brothers.

By this time I had lived with my adopted mother for several years and had become more conscious of her character, her good and not so good qualities. The students' daily behavior and disrespect disturbed me. I could not discuss my problem with anyone because it directly affected my mother. I believed it was too personal and it bothered me because I felt powerless. I had to find a way to resolve this problem by myself. The name-calling had to stop.

Chapter 10

"My name is Maria Russo"

My mother must have spoken to one of my aunts about her difficulties with my burgeoning rebelliousness. My aunt then asked me to spend a couple of weeks with her at her summer beach house on the sandy shores of Lake Erie. Her home was far enough from Fredonia to give my mother a semblance of vacation time from me. She had to have been eager for the respite, especially since she also had had a difficult school year.

The trade-off was that I was to babysit my two cousins who were adolescents. I was surprised with my aunt's request because I had no experience with caring for children and had had little interest in them, but I went willingly into a new occurrence.

My young cousins and I had no set daily activities, so we spent the day sun bathing, swimming or wandering the extensive public beaches.

One day, we chanced to walk away from our usual haunts, past the prone sun-bronzed and well-oiled bodies that littered the sands, when I spied an unusual sight. A torso of a man without arms or legs was propped against a low stone wall that was shaded by a large maple tree. He was engaged in a lively conversation with men and women who were lying on towels around him.

When I focused on the individuals relaxing under the tree, I realized that all the sunbathers had a limb missing or had some deformity. My cousins and I had inadvertently stumbled into a private institutional beach.

We slowed our pace to stare in amazement for we had never encountered anyone who was deformed. This was, for us, a world apart. Likewise, we were silently studied by the inhabitants of the shaded beach to check our reactions to their uniqueness. Out of embarrassment, we turned around and headed back for home.

As the days progressed we wandered further from the safety of my aunt's house for, as usual, my wanderlust knew no bounds.

We followed a paved walkway that veered away from the beach front. The path was easier to navigate than the beach whose sand constantly sucked our feet. It soon meandered under a stone bridge which was used by a group of boys as an overhang to view and torment the tourists. They were enjoying their sport while drinking from their cans of beer.

As we were nearing the tunnel-like opening, I was distracted by my cousins' comments. I looked down to speak to them and at the same time I heard the boys calling down to me. I didn't bother responding to their jeers and that angered one of the hecklers. I felt an object split my scalp and blood began pouring down my face. My cousins began screaming.

When I looked up at the bridge all the boys had disappeared. I searched for help and held out my bloody hands in supplication. A woman came to my aid. She put her arm around my shoulders and shepherded me to the first aid station.

I spent the remainder of my two-week hiatus healing on the beach fronting my aunt's bungalow. That vacation netted me the second of my major head injuries. Again, I was an innocent bystander in an uncontrollable event.

Chapter 11

"My name is Maria Russo"

When I entered the 10th grade I began working at Hunter's store in downtown Fredonia where they sold lunches, cigarettes, newspapers, paperback books, candy and ice cream. This job paid for my college education, improved my interpersonal skills and helped me to gain management skills. I held this job for several years. My employers, Mr. and Mrs. Hunter, were unbelievably patient, reserved, respected and involved in community events.

The following incident illustrated for me Mrs. Hunter's humor and patience. I was refilling the ketchup bottles in the store while we were speaking of inconsequential events. I had opened a large can of ketchup and was twisting the tin top to break the final connection. I must have twisted the top off too aggressively because the lid scooped up a wealth of ketchup and hurled it all over my clothes and face. It also covered Mrs. Hunter and ran down the walls and mirror. I expected her to react with anger, but all she said was, "I believe you had better head home to change."

Many years later, I was shocked to hear from Mr. Hunter that his wife had fallen victim to a debilitating disease that left her bedridden for the rest of her life. Mr. Hunter, a man who lived life to the fullest, eventually met a wealthy, European business woman whom he married. Before he moved to Italy, we would often meet and share a meal when I traveled home to visit my mother. Along with my Uncle Joe, Glen Hunter also had a great impact on my life.

Because of the couple's guidance, I continued to develop my humor, fostered a more sophisticated vocabulary and decided to involve myself in high school clubs and events.

The only negative aspect of my job at Hunter's was that I had to deal with my employer's teenage son. He had a case of raging hormones and tended to "accidently" rub against a female employee whenever he had the opportunity of passing by her. Thankfully, this subtle form of harassment stopped as soon as his sisters began working at the store.

While at Hunter's I formulated a plan to solve my mother's name-calling problem.

The game of basketball became a key venue for me to gain facial recognition in high school so to curb my mother's attackers. After a time, I became the captain of the basketball team but, unfortunately, had to retire after a year. I broke a bone in my foot while attempting a jump shot, but I benefited from my short stint with the team for I gained a reputation for aggressiveness.

Since clubs are always vying for people to play key roles, I became a treasurer of one club and the vice president of another. My sense of humor developed further and I had the common sense to avoid the type of trouble that I had encountered in my neighborhood.

My plan worked.

As I neared the end of high school, groups of students would pass my mother and me on the street and instead of calling out my mother's name they would greet us. The students were aware of my scrutiny and they were courteous and respectful toward both of us. The change in behavior, especially when passing my house, took several years, but it was well worth the wait since there was also a change in my mother's demeanor. I don't believe she was aware of my involvement in her affairs, but her behavior was more relaxed when we were attending school plays and musical events. I also benefited, for I was better equipped to deal with college life and its vagaries.

Chapter 12

"My name is Maria Russo"

I acquired a group of friends during high school who better reflected my mother's values. At hindsight, I might have easily been persuaded by others to join groups that did not value education, did not follow school rules and found pleasure in drinking and smoking, but when I was approached by the outlying groups, I would reflect on my mother's role in the school district and, invariably, made the choice that was best for me.

My new friends invited me into their homes and to their parties. One of my best friends, Peggy, was a godsend. She had a presence about her; she was down- to- earth, was knowledgeable about cars, was full of health and was fun to be with. The boys in our group were in love with her. I later discovered that she was dating two of the boys at the same time and eventually married one of them when she graduated, but she never publically acknowledged her relationship with them. I discovered the radical changes in her lifestyle when I attended our first high school reunion.

But while in high school and during the halcyon days of summer, we would spend nights racing cars on the beaches of Lake Erie, or would sit in front of a roaring bonfire while we listened to the murmur of waves, or followed the progression of stars in the sky. Surprisingly, no one in the group smoked or drank.

My friend, Bob, was a member of the group.

An Awakening

When young
The naked moon drew me
To search the fragrant nights
For a kindred soul who understood
My flights of fancy, and
Who would crave
The tides of desire.

I did not date anyone in the group, for Peggy was the main attraction. She was the comet and I was the tail, so I eagerly gathered any affection that was not absorbed by Peggy. The boys were in love with her, and since I was her closest friend, I was readily accepted.

Several of the boys went to SUNY -Fredonia at the same time as I, and they became my support group during my freshman year. We were friends and enjoyed being together. I believe that my association with these six people in high school may have also helped to resolve the situation with my mother.

Even though my new friends were clean-cut, my mother was not comfortable with the idea of my associating with them. She had met a few of my girlfriends who were on the fringes and she had met their parents, but she had never seen me in the context of the group that was composed of four boys and two girls. She also was not totally comfortable with my emerging personality, or my new-found popularity.

Without my knowledge, my mother decided to follow me on one of our outings to Lake Erie. My friends and I decided, because of our numbers, to take two cars. We had traveled several miles out of Fredonia when I spotted my mother's car behind us. I was bemused since she had never had the courage to check up on me before, but I had never given her any reason not to trust me.

As we left the outskirts of the town one of our cars died. We parked that car by the side of the road and my friends and I piled into the remaining car and resumed our journey. My mother might have thought that we were deliberately trying to trick her, but she had no choice but to continue to drive past our working vehicle. As she passed us we all yelled "Hi, Mom!" and waved.

My mother and I never discussed the above incident, but that was not unusual since we were not open with each other. She was known for her conservative and private demeanor, but I believe that she may have been embarrassed to have been caught following us.

Chapter 13

"My name is Maria Russo"

My first sexual experience was a rape and, ironically, my mother was instrumental in setting it up.

I was in high school and, because I was older, my mother trusted me to be alone at home. She had hired a local man to paint the interior of our home. Since he was there for several days he believed he had the run of the house. At one point he saw me dressed in a black slip. I had had to travel from my bedroom on the second floor to the bathroom on the first floor. He stared but did not acknowledge the situation.

Several days passed and my mother happened to be home. The man was busy painting. I had changed from school dress to casual clothing and had informed my mother that I was heading for the beach on my bike. The painter, who was in his 40's, mentioned that he lived in Dunkirk near the beach. My mother asked him if he would be willing to drive me there since he was soon leaving to head home.

I told my mother that he did not need to bother; I did not trust him since I had observed him watching me. My mother kept insisting that I take the ride to the lake, and so to avoid a confrontation that was going to make things worse, I accepted the ride.

There was little conversation as the painter and I headed for the beach. Dunkirk is several miles from Fredonia, so it did not take long to travel the distance. I noticed immediately that he deviated in his route once we arrived in the adjoining town. When I mentioned that he was going the wrong way, he stated that he needed to drop by his house to pick up some items. When I didn't budge from the front seat, because I intended to wait for him in the car, he asked me to come into the house for a minute.

As we entered his place, he grabbed my arm and roughly pulled me up the stairs to the second floor. I tried to break away, but he threatened to kill me if I did not go with him. I couldn't fathom his type of threat because I had never been manhandled since I had been adopted. He then demanded that I keep quiet and not resist as he threw me on the bed, took off my shorts and loosened his pants.

It took him no time at all to breach my body. I can still recollect his sweaty body, his reddened and grimacing face and his grunting. I laid there quietly like a stone. He may have been pleasured by his act of rape, but to me he was just a rutting male. When he realized that I was not physically reacting - crying or screaming- he told me to put on my shorts. Then, without any more conversation on his part, he took me to the beach and drove off in his car.

My first experience with forceful intercourse did not negatively affect me as it has affected many women who have experienced rape. In my case, the rape was so quick and so unexpected that it was of little consequence when compared to the violence, the bombings and the ravages of war.

I saw the same man with his wife several weeks later in Hunter's. He ordered coffee and watched me fill his order. His wife may have wondered why he scrutinized my actions so closely. I was s-o-o-o tempted to dump the entire coffeepot on his lap, but in the 60's even the police blamed the victim for enticing the man and creating the situation, so

I did and said nothing. I was underage and in high school at the time. He could have been charged with rape, but even at that young age I did not want to shame my mother or the adults whom I respected, such as Mr. and Mrs. Hunter.

My mother would have been horrified to discover that she had initiated such a traumatic event, especially since she had never dated in her life nor had ever been married. I never spoke to her about the incident or brought up her role in my first sexual experience. It would have devastated her.

Chapter 14

"My name is Maria Angela Russo"

When I was attending the Campus school as a 9th grader, my mother stopped seeing me as a servant. Because of the community's perception of the role I played in her family – her daughter – she began the process of formally adopting me and making me a citizen of the United States. I did not go through the written and oral tests that adults have to undergo today. Because of my youth and the circumstances under which I was adopted, I was automatically processed as an American citizen.

My mother now seemed to view me as a companion. Her older friends were slowly passing away or were physically incapable of traveling, so we began by traveling to

Canada to stay at Desert Lake with another set of cousins whom I called "Aunt" and "Uncle". In deference to my aunt's kind nature, I took on her first name, Angela, as my middle name.

My relative's remote camp was quiet and was situated in heavily forested wilderness. There were few roads and we could only access their cabin by crossing the lake by boat.

I have several vivid recollections of their place. I remember swimming one early morning and discovering that I was sharing the quiet waters with over a dozen black snakes. My uncle was continuously trying to kill them with an oar since they were venomous. They tended to congregate on the back steps of the porch to bask in the heat of the afternoon sun. To this day, I shudder when I remember the snakes rearing their heads preparing to strike. I found; however, that I fell in love with the open spaces, the solitude, the smell of the resin-laden Eastern white pines and the quiet tooting of loons. I still relish the clarity of a sky filled with myriad stars and the tranquility of a forest.

Spirit Name

I heard my name in the night…

In the soughing of white pines,
The lapping of clear waters on a lake's edge,
The soft hooting of a horned owl.

A nocturnal song,
Imbued with muted melodies and
Soft harmonies.

I have heard my name in the night.

My mother and I also traveled to the New England states and to the Adirondack Mountains in upper New York State. It's embarrassing to realize that it took me that long to discover that she loved nature and the mountains.

It was also amazing to realize that this formidable woman was shy and anxious when confronted with new situations involving men. For example, she had rented a room for us in a rustic Adirondack lodge in Blue Mountain village. She had closed our bedroom door and was unpacking warmer clothing when a man barged into the room. He demanded that we leave because he believed that our room was his.

My mother was paralyzed by the situation, and I just stood next to her wondering how the problem was going to be resolved. Luckily, the proprietor of the place had followed him. He gently grabbed him by the arm and ushered him to the correct room.

My mother no longer trusted the latch that secured the door, and for additional security, propped a chair under the door knob. I don't believe she slept a wink that night.

It was an eye-opener for me when we first traveled to the Blue Mountain area of the Adirondacks. My mother left me to my own devices which she rarely had done before. She elected to join a group of adults who decided to climb Blue Mountain. I stayed close to our lodging and instead canoed on Blue Mountain Lake. I had never canoed before, but the lake was calm and I stayed for safety's sake near the shore line. It was a memorable experience.

I also met a boy who was my age and he and I walked along the steep shoulder of Rt. 28 enjoying the total darkness of wilderness, stars unblemished by city lights and the freedom to speak of mutual interests.

My mother and I also attended Chautauqua Institute in western New York every Sunday. This religious retreat is known for its study of spiritualism, its music and its lectures. We benefited from a lecture conducted in the leaf-shrouded amphitheater by Margaret Mead. She was a noted American cultural anthropologist who promoted expanding the sexual mores in the people of the South Pacific, but through a traditional religious life. I was impressed, for this was my first introduction to a world-renowned speaker who was a woman.

The smell of fresh, buttered popcorn and the novelty of icy sherbet were welcome additions to Sunday afternoons filled with music and sunshine.

My mother and I discovered, through our excursions to various states, that we had an affinity for the autumn season. It was an impassioned season full of wild winds and subdued colors for both of us.

The Age of Metals

To absorb the autumn day
I walk the northern woods
To view cinereous waters
Under leaden skies.

The muted verdigris of pines
The bronze glow of mighty oaks,
Silver birches and
The golden flash of stately maples.

From the hawk's eyrie one views
A rolling carpet,
An alchemist's blend
Of burnished, metallic colors.

Chapter 15

"My name is Maria Angela Russo"

As a senior in high school, I was privy to a conversation between my mother and my guidance counselor. My mother was voicing her concern that I would not get accepted into SUNY-Fredonia. At this stage, I could converse in English at a rudimentary level, but the idioms were still a terror to understand.

For example, an individual who is not fluent with the English language may not know that there is not only a literal meaning, but also a figurative meaning to the idiom "You're pulling my leg." This confusion of nuances lasted well into my 20's, since there are numerous idioms in the English language. Nevertheless, I understood my mother's comments, but I didn't understand her apprehension. I did not want my favorite guidance counselor to question my abilities.

My mother's anxiety of my academic future disappointed me. She definitely felt that I didn't have a prayer of doing well in college. Overhearing that conversation and what it implied subconsciously prompted me as an adult to achieve above and beyond what was realistically expected of me.

It was fortunate for me that Fredonia was a college town, for it had a policy of accepting local students in its musical or educational programs. Since I possessed little innate ability in music, I opted to enroll in its teaching program. Some of my friends had already been accepted into the school's much touted music program so I had some incentive to consider SUNY-Fredonia.

I'm certain my mother did most of the grunt work, such as processing my applications and speaking with the school's agents. I do remember my interview with the school's representative. My responses and my background must have been somewhat bizarre, but I may have intrigued him enough to accept me. It also may have helped that I had attended SUNY's Campus school as a 9th grader.

Chapter 16

"My name is Maria Angela Russo"

There is an axiom, "Curiosity killed the cat." My interest in dating college- aged boys was almost my downfall.

In the summer between my high school graduation and my freshman year in college, I spent summer days with a lifeguard who monitored a section of Lake Erie's beach front. My relationship with the lifeguard opened my eyes to how others, such as his family, saw me. His family was considered upper-crust because of their wealth. As a teacher, my mother was not deemed to be in the same class.

The young man was unconcerned with my background and took me to his mansion several times for lunch. His maid served us. I had the opportunity to meet his mother, but she basically ignored me and imperiously ordered her son to complete various mundane tasks around their home. I did not feel welcomed, but it wasn't an issue with me since I knew that the relationship would end as soon as I entered college.

I enjoyed watching my boyfriend work as a lifeguard but, most of all, I craved our time at night when we would play in the water in the turbulent breakers that would tumble and push us onto the boulder-strewn shore.

During the day we would bake in the sun and would strut up and down the beach. We made a sensational-looking couple. I considered it a time to reap new experiences.

I also was dating a young man who was not attending college, but who lived and worked in town; however, there was little chemistry between us. Our relationship was going nowhere, so I moved on to experience other men my age. Unfortunately, one of these adventures backfired on me.

It was a hot and lush summer day when I noticed the black Mustang. The driver seemed to be in his 20's and was ruggedly handsome. He drove his low-slung car up and down the road that bordered the beach. He was not in casual clothing, but was dressed in a black suit which made him look like James Bond. He was an exotic bloom among the beach bums. He was an impressive specimen and I responded to his charm and conversation.

For me, it was a summer of stylishness. I had begun sewing high-end, couture clothing toward the conclusion of high school so that I could compete with the more sophisticated clothing worn by the well-heeled seniors. My bathing suit was based on a Vogue design – a two piece, chocolate- brown number that enhanced a well-endowed figure. For the late 60's, it was a very modern and daring style.

The young man and I carried on a conversation for some time about his car, where I lived, college life and life in a small town until the beach emptied and the sun began to set.

I told him that my mother was expecting me home for supper and that it would definitely take me an hour or so to get home by bike. He offered me a ride and I accepted.

We continued to talk as he drove toward Fredonia. When we got close to my street I told him to let me off on a road before my actual street. My past experience with the painter had made me apprehensive of the unknown.

He did not turn into the road that I had identified as mine but continued to drive onward. When I grabbed his arm to call his attention to his mistake, he stated that he was heading out of town toward a motel in which he was currently staying.

Without a moment's thought I opened the car door and rolled out of the car onto the street. I quickly ran into the woods that edged the road and began running from tree to tree trying to evade the car that had jumped the curb and was trying to run me down.

The car's brakes squealed and he revved the engine. He angrily cursed me as his car ran over bushes and drove between trees. I moved into denser shrub and the darkness enveloped me.

Since I was familiar with the area, for I had often roamed through this neighborhood, I soon lost him. His car did a U-turn, drove back onto the street and roared off into the night.

The woods quieted and the cicadas resumed their chirping. The ambient light from the street lamps guided my way as I wended my way home. It was one of the few times that I viewed my home and my little bedroom as a refuge.

Chapter 17

"My name is Maria Angela Russo"

SUNY – Fredonia accepted me in its teaching program. With a Bachelor's in education I could teach middle school and high school throughout the state of New York.

The college atmosphere contrasted dramatically with my time in high school. Ideas and conversations flowed; one could easily voice personal and political views without being criticized.

I continued to work at Hunter's 20 hours a week for I needed to pay college tuition and extraneous expenses. I worked, attended classes and studied either at the school library, the Student Lounge or at home.

It seemed that friends were easier to come by in a college atmosphere, but I still had the support of the cadre of friends from high school. We would meet occasionally in the Student Lounge to exchange news and to share a snack.

I was drawn to an English professor as a freshman and at the same time regained my friendship with the same biology professor who had befriended me when I was a 9th grader. It had been difficult to decide in which direction my future was heading for both men had qualities that I admired, but I eventually decided, as a sophomore, to pursue an English degree.

Chapter 18

"My name is Maria Angela Russo"

Tom was my first legitimate romantic relationship in college. He may have been the first college boy I met who did not have any excessive childhood baggage. He was even-tempered and was happy attending sporting events or walking about town.

Fredonia is a small town, so I shouldn't have been surprised that he might have somehow heard of my mother's reputation as a formidable woman.

We had gone drinking and dancing. It was past midnight and as usual he walked me home. As we stood by my front steps, I admitted that my mother might be upset at the late hour. As my mother opened the inner door, Tom took off and ran toward town. I was astonished to see Tom's headlong flight and couldn't fathom the reason for it.

I was to meet Tom the next night at a basketball game as soon as I was done studying. I waited in the bleachers in the gymnasium but did not see hide or hair of him. Eventually, I spotted his group of friends at the door and saw within the group an individual whose head and hands were swaddled in gauze bandages. The bandaged person resembled an Egyptian mummy.

The group headed in my direction. As they neared my seat one of the boys quietly identified the injured boy as Tom. To my chagrin, I was told that Tom had tripped on the curb and had landed on his face while trying to get away from my mother's influence.

I was bemused by the entire incident, but Tom took it personally. He ignored me for three weeks; it affected his ego to have his friends tease him while he was healing.

My self-image received an unusual boost in my first year of college. Music events and plays were commonplace and many students used them as a reprieve between study periods. I had decided to attend a concert after spending an afternoon in the library and was pleasantly surprised when I entered the auditorium. A male friend, who was in the music program, acknowledged my attendance by playing a solo rendition of "Maria" on his saxophone. It was an unforgettable moment for me to attend a music concert and to hear a piece of music played in my honor.

My freshman year was a heady interval for me. It was the heyday of "The Beatles" and college students filled the local bars at night to sing, drink and dance for hours. It was common in the evening to see college students sitting on the curb taking a breather or making out in the leafy darkness of the town park.

I don't drink as an adult, but as a freshman I learned to enjoy one or two glasses of Southern Comfort between bouts of exuberant dancing.

Chapter 19

"My name is Maria Angela Russo"

As a sophomore I was heading to the Student Union for a break between classes when I saw a college student sitting on the floor. He had propped himself against one of the interior columns. It was a very dark part of the large room, but I thought I recognized him as my best friend's boyfriend. I greeted him and he slurred a "Hi" back to me. I then realized that he might be drunk, even though it was the middle of the afternoon, so after introducing myself I left for my next class.

A day or so passed before I received a phone call from him. (For the sake of confidentiality I'll name him Jay). Jay asked whether I would be interested in getting together to study. Over time, he asked me to plays, lectures, musical performances and dances. On some evenings, we spent time on the banks of a local stream behind the elementary school enjoying each other and the sounds of the roiling water and the enclosing night. Our contact with nature had some disadvantages. It had been embarrassing to explain to Mr. Hunter why my legs were covered with Calamine lotion and an extreme case of poison ivy.

In high school, I did not have the time, inclination or money to attend dances, but then I had not dated much. My school clothing was adequate for the regular events, but Jay asked me to attend formal college gatherings with him, so I required a more elaborate wardrobe. The only way I could procure it was to make it.

I spent money on more intricate and expensive fabrics and used Vogue designs that were intended to create an impact. One of my creations was a two piece affair; a white crepe slip dress with spaghetti straps that was worn under a long-sleeved, jewel-necked, white, see-through cage dress that was edged at the hem with ostrich feathers. The dress was augmented with matte silver stockings and silver low-heeled pumps. There were not many occasions to wear a couture dress in a college town, but when I did wear the garment I was constantly complimented on it.

I had learned to sew in high school and it became another source of income and relaxation. I sewed the psychedelic shirts of the 60's and 70's for Jay. When my daughter grew out of diapers, Julia would be attired in outfits that often complimented mine. I earned extra money by sewing for six men who ordered detailed shirts, ties, slacks and sports jackets. My daughter, when she was attending high school, proudly wore one of my Vogue designs as a prom dress.

While Julia was an infant and then a small child, I spent hours sewing while I watched over her. I would listen to her breathe as she slept in the night. I found solace in the rhythmic push and pull of the foot trestle of a Singer sewing machine, the creative energy spent on designing a garment and the small profit gained from satisfied customers.

Chapter 20

"My name is Maria Angela Russo"

Jay and I meshed. We began a love affair and by the summer, in order to save money, we moved into an apartment. Because we were enrolled in some of the same classes and were both in the same field we were able to occasionally see each other. We also had the same advisor whom we both respected.

Jay's attitude and behavior in our Chaucer course disturbed me for it showed me another aspect of his personality. I spent quite a bit of effort doing the classwork and trying to understand the Old English script. Jay was comatose during the class; he seemed to be nursing a hangover every time the class met.

He slept through the entire course, and with only six people in the class it was pretty obvious to the professor his level of interest in what she was teaching. Jay never excused his behavior, and because the relationship was new I was willing to accept that he either partied hard or drank excessively.

I was attracted; however, to his intensity outside of class. I believed that we both needed each other and that we shared similar attitudes and outlooks. We each had survived dysfunctional and traumatic childhoods. Jay was fostered in 13 homes. He hinted at abuse, neglect, abandonment and excessive drinking in his family. He also didn't seem to have any financial resources. As a freshman and sophomore, he ate only one meal a day and that was at a local buffet where he could refill his plate countless times.

Because I believed I could help his living conditions and his emotional state, I asked him if he wished to marry. I only gave my mother a couple of weeks' notice that Jay and I were to marry. Jay's mom- believed that we were marrying because I was pregnant. She surprised me with this fact when I was in my 30's and had been Jay's wife for 11 years. It was difficult convincing her that her belief had no merit, but she was extremely Catholic and she felt that we had lived in sin.

I don't recall any conversations with Jay's mother about the wedding. My mother made all the plans for the reception. Jay's mother had to have orchestrated the wedding ceremony since her two brothers were directly involved.

Jay's family was Irish/German, and was very conservative and very religious. We had a full-blown Catholic wedding ceremony. There were three priests officiating the wedding which made it a High Mass. The only time I had viewed such an elaborate service was when I was an orphan. A bishop from the Vatican had conducted a High Mass for the parishioners at the church connected to the orphanage. It isn't often that priests prostrate themselves during a mass or chant the entire service; it has to be a special pretext, but it made sense since two of the priests were Jay's uncles.

My mother had hurriedly rented a banquet room at "The White Inn" which was the best hotel and restaurant in Fredonia and she had invited some of her friends to the reception. Jay and I had only invited my maid of honor and his best man to attend us.

I did not know anyone in Jay's family and I do not recall any conversations with any member of his extensive family. Actually, very few may have shown up for the wedding ceremony and the reception. They may have shown their displeasure by being absent. Years later, one of Jay's sisters told me his family believed that I had forced him to marry me. From Jay's perspective, that may have been true.

The wedding was small and informal. I had never had any desire for a wedding dress or a lavish affair, so I wore a white brocade suit, white pumps and a white lace mantilla. Jay and I spent a short period of time at the reception, left for our apartment and attended classes the next day. We never had a honeymoon; we had too hectic of a life.

I have no pictures of the wedding except of one with the wedding party. It would be interesting to know who attended, but with the birth of a daughter, a divorce, my mother's death and the passage of time the event has lost its significance.

Chapter 21

"My name is Maria Beurmann"

Jay, by associating with me and a close male friend, became more confident and outgoing during his last two years of college. He became involved in the protests against the Vietnam War. He did not see the irony of his actions since he had avoided the draft because he was married and I was newly pregnant.

As a junior, I continued to attend classes, but ended my job at Hunter's. Most of the students who knew me did not realize I was carrying, but thought that I had gained weight and was just plump.

Jay became Editor-in-Chief of the college paper at SUNY-Fredonia in 1965. My daughter, as an infant, became the school's mascot and her baby picture graced the paper next to the banner headline.

It was a frigid winter. I remember walking several miles each day to attend classes while pushing a baby carriage through inches of snow.

Jay seemed to exhibit a younger spirit as his junior year advanced. It was as if he had not had a childhood and desired some fun. He involved himself in some questionable stunts.

He and his friends decided to cut down a large spruce that was planted on the college president's front lawn. They took the tree to the friends' dorm and festooned it with Christmas ornaments for all to view. He also tweaked a banner headline on the newspaper to read, "President Johnson Has Got His Piece." Jay was called in by the college president to explain the reason for the title. The play on words caused quite a stir since the paper was distributed not only at the college but throughout the community.

College women became interested in Jay because of his capers. They began visiting his school office at all hours. I actually benefited from their visits because they volunteered to babysit my daughter while I attended classes. I wasn't; however, pleased at the change in Jay's behavior and attitude.

When Jay began to return to our house after 2:00 a.m., I became concerned. I knew that there were deadlines; the newspaper had to be put to bed and many people were involved in its production and distribution, but by now my childhood home that my mother rented to us was stultifying. It seemed that I spent hours sitting in a rocking chair nursing Julia, or sewing clothes. I found myself, in the early hours of the morning, watching goldfish and guppies swim in circles in their tank.

Raising a child 24/7 is difficult and added to that is the effort invested in attending classes during the day and completing homework at night. I was exhausted and depressed.

Finally, I reached my limit. I was resentful of the excessive time Jay spent with his friends, the college women and the newspaper. I gave him an ultimatum; either spend time at home helping raise our daughter, or the marriage was finished.

I felt that he was living a more enjoyable lifestyle than I was and I resented the fact that he did not earn a salary as Editor-in-Chief, especially since he spent so much time in his office. He was surrounded by vibrant people his own age and he was living rent-free in my mother's house. I believed that

Jay's only concerns were his classes, his friends and the newspaper.

My husband changed his routine to accommodate me and began to spend more time at home; however, he invited his newspaper staff to our house to discuss business. Invariably, these meetings turned into parties that my husband and I seemed to fund. I was not happy to see inert and drunken bodies lying on our lawn after a night's festivities.

Surprisingly, Julia survived the year's bedlam. Even though we played rock and roll music during the parties, she was often lulled to sleep by classical music that softly played in her room throughout the night. She did not object to being the center of attention when she was awake.

Chapter 22

"My name is Maria Beurmann"

I covered my tuition and my day-to-day expenses for my first two years of college through my job at Hunter's and through my scholarship. I had never considered applying for loans. My husband; however, had paid for his freshman and sophomore years with loans, so we decided to use his method of payment to get us through the last two years of college.

We were poor.

Jay's best friend decided to bring his wife, Paula, and his daughter from the New York City area to Fredonia. It caused a stir since he had claimed for a couple of years to be single and had been dating a score of college women. Both families got along famously and enjoyed each other's company.

The four adults would sit around the dining room table thinking of ways to survive. On weekends, we began searching the countryside for food. It was desperation that caused us to drive from farm to farm in Fredonia and the outlying towns. Jay and I had been used to the lack of food, but the other couple had not faced that hardship in NYC since their parents, to a degree, had supported them financially.

The first farm we scavenged was one that raised cabbages. Unfortunately, we had to quickly drive away because the farmer began shooting at us.

We decided to steal corn so to freeze it. It took some time to fill the inside of the car with ears of corn, but on the way out of the enclosed farm I shucked an ear and discovered that it was animal corn. We immediately threw the inedible corn out of the windows.

When we arrived at the farm's front gate, a N.Y. State Trooper stopped us and asked to search our car. He had received a call from the farmer that thieves were stealing his corn. When the policeman searched our car, all he saw were leaves and corn silk. The policeman was suspicious, but there was no actual proof that we had committed a crime.

Another time, we decided to raid a local factory in Fredonia that imported vegetables in its semi-trucks. We knew that they had had a shipment of green beans, so the four of us parked our car flush to the fence and the two men jumped the fence. The two women, a pregnant Paula and I, were to pretend that we were a couple making out in the back seat. It was difficult not to laugh at the situation, but since it was pitch black in the car, we hoped that no one would discover our ruse.

Paula and I watched our husbands scale the side of the truck, climb in and begin filling bags with green beans. It was in the middle of the night, so the guys had trouble seeing what they were doing. When the lights of another truck swept over our car, our husbands began scrambling out of the truck bed. Jay jumped first and landed on the ground. Paula's husband couldn't see the ground because it was dark, so he jumped but landed on top of Jay. Beans went flying everywhere and both men attempted to gather whatever they could of the remaining beans. It was a fruitless task, so they quickly scrambled over the fence and jumped into the car.

Because of our lack of funds, I became a master connoisseur of hot dogs and hamburgers. Since these were the cheapest meats during the 60's, I learned to fix both in multiple ways. It took all my ingenuity to provide cheap but filling meals the first years of our marriage.

Chapter 23

"My name is Maria Beurmann"

I had not had much contact with my mother since my wedding day, so I had not had a chance to tell her how much I appreciated all that she had done for me. Because I had not contacted her, she was irritated at both of us. She was further aggravated when I gave birth to my daughter, Julia, and had not invited her to attend me at the hospital. My mother did not realize that the hospital frowned on having family members in the delivery room. She felt that I had deliberately kept her out, so she did not make the effort to see her granddaughter until Julia was over three months old.

We never had had a relationship where my mother would drop in to see us, even though we rented her house, and because we were so involved in school events and were raising our daughter, my husband and I did not visit her.

Jay, likewise, had a lukewarm relationship with his family. Since his mother had given up her four children to foster homes, time and distance had separated everyone in his family. I found out many years later, when his mother would visit my home during the autumn season that she would have liked more contact with Jay. However, because of the trauma of his childhood, he had become insular and reserved.

Within a month or two after our marriage, Jay decided to visit during a weekend his mother, his uncle and his high school friends who lived in the western part of the state near Rochester, New York.

His intent was to leave my daughter and me with his mother and uncle so that he could spend several hours with his friends. I had had little contact with his mother or uncle and I felt that being left alone with them for hours was an imposition to everyone.

Both Jay's mother and uncle; however, were very gracious. They opened their home to us and served us fillet mignon for dinner with baked potatoes and peas. Both Jay and I were used to greater quantities of food for each meal so we ended up going to McDonalds for another dinner. We laughed about the irony of being served the best of meats, but ending up with a meal from a restaurant that served junk food. It was just that neither of us could handle going hungry again.

When Jay left to visit his friends, I put Julia to bed and moved into the living room to visit my mother-in-law and Jay's uncle. They had steadily been drinking whiskey during dinner and continued to drink as the hours passed. Something superfluous was brought up in their conversation and they both started hitting and yelling at each other. The altercation moved outside to the porch and the slapping and pushing continued.

It had started snowing in the early evening hours so when Jay's mother and uncle stepped out on the porch they began losing their balance and began to slide about. I became concerned because both adults were in their pajamas and the lack of traction on their slippers made them crash into the garbage containers. I tried to calm them by attempting to usher them back into the house, but my inane conversation did nothing to soothe them and they continued to flail about. Eventually, I gave up and went back into the house. I had very little history or contact with these two people so I knew I had no influence on their behavior.

When Jay returned I gave him chapter and verse of the incident, but he had seen this behavior so often that he shrugged it off. I got angry at him. I had seen many college students who were drunk, but I had never seen excessively drunk adults. It affected my attitude and my future relationship with them.

Chapter 24

"My name is Maria Beurmann"

Jay and I managed to survive the last two years of college and we graduated in 1966 with Bachelor degrees in English. I had been a student teacher at Dunkirk High School in 1965 and I had had a difficult time. The English teacher that I was assigned to was a master teacher with years of teaching experience. I believe she hoped for a person who was as qualified as she was. It was obvious that she did not get what she hoped for, because during one of her classes she stopped my lesson and yelled "If you don't teach like I teach, then you won't teach at all."

Thankfully, she didn't have a heart attack while I was her student teacher, but the experience was so traumatic that I lost 15 pounds.

When my student teaching ended, the master teacher recommended me for a half-year teaching position in the same school. I became a substitute teacher for a woman who was on maternity leave.

As proof that my student teaching experience was unique, my college supervisor asked me to be on a college panel to present another viewpoint - that student teaching could be a negative experience. I enjoyed being on the panel, but I was just glad that the student teaching was over and done with.

Before student teaching at Dunkirk High School, my mother had given me the opportunity to gain some experience in her middle school. She asked me to cover her English classes and study halls while she attended a three-day English conference. My respect for her increased a thousand-fold when I completed the three-day stint.

I had a professor in college who advised his classes that a teacher had to start off at the beginning of the school year as a strict teacher. He added that an instructor can always become less strict as the school year progressed, but it was impossible to start off as a pal to the students and then become more exacting.

That was the philosophy I followed when I covered for my mother. She taught five English classes of 7th and 8th graders daily and then had to supervise a study hall in the school's auditorium. I entered each class, introduced myself to the students, stated the rules and my goals and then mentioned the punishment if they did not comply.

Much to my mother's credit and skill, no student caused any problems during the entire three days. I had been extremely apprehensive substituting for my mother and monitoring a hundred students in the study hall. For her sake, I wanted to do well. My mother had never been effusive with her praise or comments, and to this day I don't remember her critiquing me or mentioning the experience.

Chapter 25

"My name is Maria Beurmann"

Jay and I had begun job hunting before we graduated in 1966 and we both obtained jobs by the beginning of the next school year. My husband landed a job with his brother-in-law at his business place and I obtained a position as an English teacher in a private, Ukrainian middle school near Rochester, New York.

It took me some time to get used to the courtesy shown by the teaching nuns, the lay teachers and the students. Everyone, except for me, greeted each other every morning with an Ukrainian prayer. I happily began to acclimate myself to a community that held education in the highest regard and who sacrificed time and money to obtain qualified teachers and quality instructional materials for its students.

I was the highest paid teacher in the school. Five thousand dollars a year is peanuts today, but it helped my husband and me to pay the bills and to put food on the table.

Again, I depended on traditional methods to teach my students. I aimed to be tough but fair and, thankfully, I was given the resources and the support of the administration.

An incident that showed the school's respect for education occurred a month or so after I began teaching my 8th grade classes.

I had a student who was the epitome of an excellent student. He was articulate, bright and had a sense of humor. These qualities made him a natural leader in the classroom, but he reveled in his humor to the point where he saw himself as the class clown. He became so disruptive that he affected my teaching and disturbed the other students' learning. I called his home and asked his parents to meet with me and their son after school. I expected to see both parents, but only the father and son appeared.

The parent waited patiently while I explained my concerns. The father was a short, wiry man who was over-shadowed by his son's height. The father slowly took off his leather belt and asked his son to lie on his stomach over a student's desk.

When I realized what the father intended, I backed away and moved to stand behind my desk. I wasn't certain if he planned to come after me when he finished with his son.

The son knew what to expect because he laid passively on the desk. He did not cry out or make a sound as his father struck him repeatedly with his belt. When he was done, the father faced his son and in broken English stated:

"I do not work to have you fool around in class. Education is important."

He then turned toward me and apologized for his son's behavior.

I had never expected the father's actions, so I was dumbfounded, but the student showed a marked improvement in his behavior, and he became one of my best pupils.

I have worked as a teacher across New York State in various schools – urban, suburban, resort, rural, open, and at Union College and I never again have experienced the father's love of learning or the support that I received from that parent.

That year was also unique because race riots were prevalent throughout the USA and, especially, at Bull's Head in Rochester. I rode public transportation to and from school and when I reached our neighborhood at Bull's Head, I passed gutted stores and looters At night, we had to contend with police cars being flipped and set on fire and guns being discharged in the neighborhood. It was so perilous a time that Jay bought a rifle to protect his family. Thankfully, we never had a need for firepower.

Jay was not happy with his job or our living conditions, so we began to search for other job opportunities away from the mayhem we were experiencing.

Chapter 26

"My name is Maria Beurmann"

We moved to the Finger Lakes region and found a large lakehouse on the shores of Keuka Lake in the community of Penn Yan. Penn Yan is known for its wines and for its ambiance as a resort area. The monthly rent for the multi-room place was ridiculously cheap, but we had to wait until the winter to discover the reason for the inexpensive rent.

The house had been built as a summer resort property and had over 12 rooms, so the heating system was almost non-existent. When we received our first energy bill, the amount was so high that we immediately called our landlord to complain. He knew that we had a legitimate complaint so he cut the monthly rental by half.

The house edged Keuka Lake. We could use the beach and the canoes in the boathouse. We spent the ice-free months crossing the lake in a canoe, watching the ducks and admiring the sunsets. We skated on the lake in winter amid the booming of shifting ice sheets. The space and quiet of the wine country was idyllic after the chaos of Rochester's urban life.

I procured a job teaching English at the Penn Yan Middle School. The administration, especially the English Department Chair, welcomed me with open arms. She shared my sense of humor and was open to different ideas. It was one of the best schools that I have experienced. It promoted learning with few restrictions.

One incident stood out the year I was there. Another teacher and I had established a friendship and our classes recognized and enjoyed the rapport between us.

The teacher of the other English class of 7th and 8th graders had a large fish tank in her room. One of the fish died. I convinced my class that we should hold a funeral for the fish and incorporate the event within our poetry unit.

I had participated in another fish funeral while attending SUNY – Fredonia. My husband and I and about half of our class staged a procession and carried the fish in a traditional coffin throughout the campus. The community saw it as frivolous and a waste of time, but it was great fun.

My middle school students decorated a blackboard with colorful construction paper and posted their poems to the fish. We then assembled a coffin out of a shoebox and carried it from our room to the other teacher's classroom. My students were instructed to assume mournful visages as we carried the coffin aloft. We then individually read our poems, odes or sonnets in honor of the heroic fish.

The teacher, for whom we had staged the show, thought our gesture was hilarious and appreciated the work behind the poetry and the display. The two day affair was valued by both teachers and students as a break in the routine and a show of solidarity.

Jay, meanwhile, had obtained his first English teaching job in an adjacent school district. The new job seemed to be going well, but then he frequently mentioned a red-headed young student. At first, he viewed her favorably and humorously, but as the weeks passed he saw her as a problem. He had chosen to make friends with the high school student and she had begun to abuse the classroom dynamics. His interest in teaching quickly deteriorated when his control of the classroom worsened. Jay's goal changed from wanting to teach to entering a graduate program in Library Science at SUNY-Albany. He decided to become a librarian.

Our lease on the rental property was up at the end of the school year, so Jay applied to Albany's graduate program and I sent out applications for an English teaching position in the tri-city area of Albany/Schenectady and Troy, New York. We were slowly moving across the state.

My chief concern with any move was to search for a reputable sitter for Julia. One of my relatives had watched her while we lived in Fredonia, and we found dependable caretakers in Rochester and Penn Yan, but now I had to scour the telephone books for a new living arrangement and a new child sitter in the Albany area. A move always proved to be a hectic time for us and a disruptive time for Julia.

Chapter 27

"My name is Maria Beurmann"

I have been fortunate in acquiring teaching positions. I have strong people skills, I research a school that interests me and I have a unique background, so I usually make a favorable impression during an interview.

Jay began his library studies at SUNY-Albany in the late 60's and I acquired a high school teaching job at Averill Park, N.Y. I was quickly hired; I may have looked young, but my teaching experiences across the state and my references from former employers made me more desirable. Fortunately, I did not have to depend on a reference from the master teacher with whom I student taught.

At Averill Park I was blessed with a class that had an innate esprit de corps. This class was an instructor's dream.

The time was right for, in the late 60's, the "Age of Aquarius" was ushering in new values of love, brotherhood, unity and integrity. The high school students were hungry and open to new ideas. My ideal class contained many artistic students who worked to create a school-wide literary magazine – the first of its kind.

The students compiled and intermixed poetry, short stories and art sketches. The books were bound with a leather thong and distributed throughout the school. Even though it was created with heavy construction paper, the inner creative works were impressive. The students and their parents appreciated the final product for it represented the creative ingenuity of the students.

I had to follow the English syllabus for the majority of my classes, but I had the opportunity to branch out by teaching unique electives to 11th and 12th graders.

I taught Black Studies through novels and short stories, integrated with another teacher the history, literature and songs of the Civil War period and with another incorporated poetry, songs and literary works that reflected the Vietnam War. I was also the advisor for the high school yearbook.

The yearbook turned out to be one of the most creative and artistic yearbooks that the school had ever seen. The professional photographer followed my plans to incorporate within the book's pages the fish eye lens, creative uses of black and white contrasts, an artistic design that introduced each new section, the use of different colors to herald a new segment and a mosaic framework for all the photos.

Even though the fish eye lens was the most expensive and the most radical or progressive of the photo techniques, I received complaints because it was unfamiliar.

While I was taking a coffee break in the Teachers' Lounge, the football coach stormed in to berate me because the football team's picture was not a traditional photo with the players posed in a linear pattern. He was abusive and public about what he thought of the pictorial setup.

My students and I had invested days and nights over a period of several months planning, meeting, and fashioning what we considered an artistic marvel. He didn't seem at all appreciative that we had highlighted his team through the fish-eye lens, so I told him,

"I'm going to put two words at the bottom of the team picture. The first starts with "F" and the second is "You!"

With that I strode out of the room. The silence was thunderous behind me.

I never heard another word from any adult, but from a creative perspective the finished product was a work of art.

It was an enlightening and exciting first and second year of teaching at this suburban/rural school.

"No man can reveal to you aught but that which already lies half asleep in the dawning of your knowledge.

The teacher who walks in the shadow of the temple, among his followers, gives not of his wisdom, but rather of his faith and his lovingness.

If he is indeed wise he does not bid you to enter the house of wisdom, but rather leads you to the threshold of your mind."

The Prophet   by Kahlil Gibran

Because of the unusual methods that I used to teach my Black Studies course, the president of the school board allowed her daughter to take a day's field trip to Spanish Harlem in New York City. Out of the 30 students who were enrolled in my Black Studies class only two students joined me on the trip. Parents had been informed of the benefits of the trip, but the field trip was too radical of an action for this conservative community.

The president's daughter was advised to cover her blond hair when we arrived in Spanish Harlem. Our guide – a graduate student from SUNY-Albany - had emphasized that we should not draw any additional attention from the residences of NYC. We heartily complied since the trip might hold some unpleasant surprises.

We were startled by the men who smeared mud on our front window and then asked to be paid for that move. Since our guide was a Spanish-American young adult we were not often hassled by the street people.

It was an edifying experience for the three of us. My students were better able to understand and to draw more informed conclusions of the daily obstacles and stultifying experiences that faced many of the characters in the novels they were required to read in my English literature classes.

It was a contentious year. At the end of the school year, a few parents complained about the novels and non-fiction works that we had been using in our English classes. Surprisingly, the main complaints originated from the town's local pulpits. The ministers read passages to their parishioners from our assigned readings, such as <u>Catcher In The Rye</u> and from non-fiction works, such as <u>Black Like Me</u>. A meeting was convened in the high school auditorium and several parents vehemently protested that the books we assigned were smutty and obscene. The English department, as a group, defended its choice of books.

The discussions and aspersions went on for hours and then days. At the end of the inflammatory discussions, one of the English teachers asked an irate parent if she had read the book. The parent had the grace to admit that she had not read <u>Catcher In The Rye</u>, but had only read the parts that her daughter had marked.

The book that I taught, <u>Soul On Ice</u>, was not even discussed because the community was not open to racial topics. When one of my students invited an African-American graduate from SUNY-Albany to speak on black/white issues, my student received death threats.

The nine members of the English Department, except for one teacher, left Averill Park at the end of the school year in search of more open-minded school districts.

That was a tumultuous period of time and I realized I needed a break from teaching. I had become interested in

programs that promoted more individualized instruction for
I found that there was a sizeable group of students in Averill
Park who were not capable of reading at grade level. I
decided to apply and enroll in a Master's degree program in
Reading at SUNY-Albany.

Chapter 28

"My name is Maria Beurmann"

SUNY-Albany is noted for its graduate reading program. I appreciated working with one specific professor during my year in the Master's program. His nickname was "No-A-Sipay", for his practice of giving very few "A's" as grades. The final project for his course was to use a lengthy reading formula that he published to determine a student's reading level or ability. Since I was volunteering at the Washington Open School in Schenectady, I selected a student whom I hoped had reading concerns and was not at grade level.

The project took about twenty hours to complete. The analysis was extensive and thorough in depicting the area or reading skill the student needed to work on.

It was a week before the final exam. I attended class to submit my final project. I had just spoken about the results of my work to a couple of students who were in my class. I had admitted to them that my test subject did not have a reading deficiency. They mentioned that they had had a similar result with their students.

As the professor was collecting the 20 page missives from the class, I brought up my results. The teacher paused and looked at me. I knew that there were others in the class that had a similar dilemma and I was expecting them to say something, but no one supported my findings or statement.

I asked, in the deafening silence,

"Do I have to select another student and do the project over again?"

The professor did not answer. He continued to look at me. I realized that my study time for the final exam was going to be severely curtailed.

I selected another student from Schenectady's Open School and went through the entire process during the week I should have been preparing for the final exam. Thankfully, the student was deficient in reading skills and I was able to apply the professor's diagnostic tests toward my findings. I successfully submitted the final project.

I did not receive an "A" as a final mark for the class, since the final exam proved to be challenging, but completing the project and meeting the professor's expectations greatly benefited me several years later.

Chapter 29

"My name is Maria Beurmann"

Jay became the Assistant to the Director of the Albany
Library System. He thoroughly enjoyed his new job.
Unfortunately, our relationship was losing its appeal for both
of us. He was focused on his new profession and I was
absorbed in raising Julia, running the household, attending
school and sewing.

As an assistant to the director, Jay was responsible for
attracting speakers to various library functions. Some
speakers came from quite a distance, so Jay and I would feed
and entertain them at our home. I learned to cook exotic
meals, such as Beef Wellington and Baked Alaska.

We also were renovating our home with the intent of
selling it and gaining a profit. Since I would soon receive my

Master's in Reading, I was in the process of finding a job teaching reading in the Albany area. The stress of juggling all my responsibilities was too much for me to handle and I lost a fetus.

Unfortunately, when I aborted, Julia was keeping me company in my bedroom; I had not been feeling well, so I had spent the day in bed. When I ejected the fetus the bed became drenched with blood. Julia was stricken silent by the sight. She could not understand at her age why her mother was sobbing at the sight of the blood. She just watched me cry as I held her close. I was heartbroken, but I had taken on too much. It was time to set priorities.

Chapter 30

"My name is Maria Beurmann"

Early in the 1970's I found a job teaching Reading at Hackett Jr. High in Albany. It was my first experience in an urban setting where the student population was mainly African-American.

The school was in the midst of race riots. My first view of the school's interior was to see students fighting in the halls. Even the principal of the school had been swept in the middle of a melee by the rioting students. I learned to crowd the lockers during the school year to avoid the brawls as I passed from class to class.

There were reasons for the discontent, especially for the African-American students. Grades and programs were skewed toward the white students. Since I primarily taught minority adolescents, I was privy to what my students covered in their core classes and the grades they received.

I believe that the school system was attempting to help my students succeed in their classes by providing them with lower readability materials, but at the end of the year these same students were required to take the same final tests that the more advanced students were given. Of course, most of the minority students failed the tests that were based on the more difficult instructional materials.

I had an unwelcome experience the year I taught at Hackett. I must have a penchant for unusual experiences, or like a magnet must attract unusual events.

My classroom was on the third floor behind the school's auditorium. The three reading teachers were housed in these back rooms because they dealt with individualized instruction and taught only three or four students at a time.

It was a dark and lonely trek from my room to the back entrance of the school at the end of the day. It didn't help to know that former teachers had been raped by men who had climbed the exterior walls of the school to get to the third floor. The exterior walls had niches that served as an artistic design, but a good climber could use them as steps.

It had been a day when everything had gone wrong; the students were not prepared with materials, a student didn't show up for class, a meeting had been scheduled with an uncooperative parent - that type of day.

The school day had ended. It was about 3:30 p.m. and it seemed that everyone had left the building. I began walking down the stairs to the auditorium. To save money and energy, the lights in the auditorium were few and dim.

I was half-way down the center aisle when a tall, black man stepped out from behind a column to block my way. It had been such a rotten day that all I could think of was, "What now?"

I looked up at the man and shrugged. He stared down at me and shrugged back. He then moved back behind the column. I kept walking toward the back of the auditorium, walked down the exit steps and moved toward my car.

The panic and shaking started when I reached my car. I had not really been analyzing the confrontation when it was happening, but when I was past the event I realized what might have occurred.

I called Jay and I cried and blathered about what had occurred. When I later mentioned the incident to a police officer who taught a local self-defense class, he stated that I had prevented anything harmful from happening because I had broken the man's pattern of behavior. He expected me to scream, cry or run like many women would have. Because I had just looked at him and shrugged, he didn't know how to respond, so he sought to hide and return to his original stance…perhaps waiting for his next victim.

Chapter 31

"My name is Maria Beurmann"

The early 70's was to prove a very painful time for both my daughter and me. Jay and I had grown apart. He had created a new world for himself with a position that provided him self-esteem and satisfaction.

I had survived a grueling year at Hackett and was ready for a change. Both of us had set new goals for ourselves.

Albany may be the capital of New York State, but it's a small town. My daughter's caretaker, as an act of kindness, told me that she had seen Jay downtown in the park with a young woman. He was kissing and embracing her. Gradually, other friends spoke of his dalliances with the same woman. Ironically, I had invited his new interest to dinner with her current partner before I discovered her connection with my husband. She worked for him so the transition from employee to girlfriend didn't take much effort.

Please…I was not innocent at the time, for there were men whom I was attracted to in Averill Park, but not much came from those friendships.

Jay and I had been married for approximately 11 years and we were both restless. I believe we reflected a song that was popular in the early 70's – "Is This All There Is." When I was in the house or in bed with my husband, I always felt so alone.

It was suggested by one of our friends that we meet with a marriage counselor, but we both had little faith in our marriage surviving even with professional assistance. I knew Jay still loved me, but he could not refute the fact that he also loved the younger woman.

It was a mutual decision that I care for Julia when we divorced. Jay was involved in a new relationship with a woman who had her own issues, so I did not believe he or his lifestyle could handle a seven-year-old girl.

Jay joined the army. As a joke, I would tell friends that to get away from me he had to join the Foreign Legion. I would also joke that I had lost 155 pounds when I got a divorce. When the person glanced at my body, I would add "I lost my husband." Sometimes, humor is the only cure for a painful event.

Jay and I were scarcely speaking, but I wondered why he joined the army at his age. He did well in the army and received awards for his scholastic achievements, but the army reneged on its promise to provide him with a place in the officer's training school. He quit after a year or two.

I can't fault him on his ability to rebound. He entered a Master's degree program in Engineering and did well in his new field. He had two children with his new partner, married her and moved to another state.

Julia felt abandoned by her father. As she grew older, she would spend some summers with him and his family, but she felt that he favored his new children.

When Julia was with me, through the school year or during the summer vacations, I would drag her fighting and kicking into my new activities: climbing mountains, hiking, camping and biking.

Chapter 32

"My name is Maria Beurmann"

Before Jay and I divorced, as an attempt to slow the growing rift in our marriage, Jay suggested a 150-mile bike trip that would begin in Albany, traverse the Lake George area and finally end in the rural area of Altamont, New York.

We were prepared with the best equipment: 15-speed bikes, maps, pannier bags, a tent, a stove, wet weather gear and food for several days.

Jay and I should have had our heads examined, because Julia was only seven or eight years old and was not used to such strenuous activity. It had to have been a traumatic and miserable experience for her.

The three of us followed back roads during our extensive trek and eventually landed in a wooded area in the

Altamont countryside. We set up camp near a small stream. Unfortunately, we were not aware that the area was a local meeting place for a group of young men. We should have been tipped off by the six-pack of beer that was cooling in the purling waters of the stream.

Night was approaching and we were preparing for sleep when two young men appeared. One of the men was definitely a Mongoloid since his head was distended beyond the normal size. He was brutish looking. They both began to verbally catalogue our equipment.

"Nice tent."

"I could use a good stove."

"What speed are those bikes?"

I began to panic, especially when the second man began flipping a hunting knife in the air. I had seen the movie "Deliverance" and the men's actions and conversations were starting to evoke the movie's scenes.

Both men sat down near us and began to open the beer cans that had cooled in the stream. They finished their drinks and departed with the statement

"We'll see you later."

I had put Julia to bed in the tent. Now, I woke her up and Jay and I scrambled to pack all our equipment on our bikes. We quickly headed for the graveled country road.

The night was pitch-black. Even the starlight didn't help as we tried to navigate toward the miniscule town. As we wobbled down the road, we passed two figures walking up the same road. We edged by them as furtively as possible and heard one of the men call out,

"Heh, where are you going?"

We sped up.

There was a firehouse at the outskirts of the town. We quickly pushed our bikes behind the building under some large bushes, set up camp and tried to get a couple of hours of undisturbed sleep.

My poor daughter; that summer of adventure held one more surprise for her.

Again we were exploring another area away from Albany and Jay was biking far ahead of us on a country road. It was a scorcher of a day and nearing the noon hour. We had been riding all morning and I knew that Julia and I needed a break to relax and to eat lunch.

I directed Julia to pull over on the shoulder, but her bike's wheels caught on the rough edge of the road. She lost her balance and careened into the middle of the public road.

I could hear a car rushing toward her, but I kept my focus on her because I was expecting her to be hit. The car did partially strike her, but the bike was totaled.

I rushed to her as she stood immobilized in the center of the road and ran my hands all over her body looking for broken bones. The bike was destroyed, but I couldn't believe the miracle. The only injury she sustained was a bent pinkie finger.

It sounds now like a joke, but the driver, a doctor, was rushing to catch a train. He was rightfully very attentive toward my daughter. He called for an ambulance and came with us to the hospital.

It's not rational, but I still get angry that Jay was not with us and did not view the potential disaster until we had been loaded on the ambulance. For me, it was a major fracture in our relationship.

Chapter 33

"My name is Maria Beurmann"

While teaching at Hackett Jr. High School I received a call from the Director of Reading at Niskayuna High School; a school that was touted as a National School of Excellence. He asked me if I were interested in coming in for an interview. I told him that I was currently working at Hackett and that I was not looking for another teaching position.

The Albany school system was notorious at that time for firing all of its teachers at the end of the school year and rehiring whomever it needed for the following September. It was the Superintendent's method of getting rid of the "dead wood."

To be safe, I called the Superintendent's office and spoke to the secretary and asked her if I would still have my teaching position in September. She didn't know how to answer my question because very few teachers called the school during the summer months to ask about their jobs.

I mentioned that I had received a call from Niskayuna for an interview and asked her if I should accept it. Again, she did not know how to respond, but in her attempt to answer my question gave me the nod.

I contacted Niskayuna's Director of Reading to set up a time to meet. I brought to the interview copies of my system of instruction that I had used at Hackett and visual aids, such as test scores, that showed the success the students achieved while in my reading programs. During a lull in the conversation I asked him why he had called me. He told me that he had contacted the SUNY- Albany Reading Department and asked the Chair of the department for names of students who would fit the Niskayuna teacher's profile. My former professor, Dr. Sipay, recommended me for the Niskayuna position. Within a few days I received a call from the Director offering me a job as the high school reading teacher.

It took the Superintendent's office in Albany three weeks into the school year to contact me to ask where I was. I mentioned what had transpired during the summer vacation. The individual suggested that I send a letter to the Albany Board of Education to explain why I was not teaching at Hackett. I did write that letter, but did not hear a word of thanks or an excuse.

Chapter 34

"My name is Maria Beurmann"

The Niskayuna School District treated me extremely well. I had limitless resources, a large room, money that I could spend on materials that I selected. It also allowed me to attend yearly reading conferences in Albany and at the Concord Hotel in the Catskill Mountains. I taught there for 14 years and at one point was offered the position of Director of Reading for the district.

I turned down the honor because there were reading teachers in the district who had more experience teaching reading and who were more familiar with the politics of the school system.

I was a one-man-band in the high school reading department. I provided individualized instruction to about 60 students per week. I primarily worked with students who had reading disabilities, but I expanded my influence by teaching students from foreign countries who were required to live in Niskayuna for a year. They were the most challenging of all my students because they often could not speak much English, plus they were unfamiliar with the mores of our country. I was fascinated by these students, their cultures and their attitudes toward education. They often represented the elite of their country so they were excited to be in the United States. They tended to rapidly learn to speak English once they immersed themselves in our culture.

Not all of the foreign exchange students were compliant. One young woman, who was required to join the Israeli army once she fulfilled her obligation to Niskayuna, threw a student's heavy desk at me because I told her that she was not up to grade level in her reading when she was first assigned to my class.

I still communicate and receive Christmas cards from a young woman who lives in the Netherlands. She still vividly recalls the hikes into the Adirondack Mountains with the Niskayuna Outing Club. Her moniker for me was and still is "Brown Bear."

I also taught speed reading to several adult classes. Men who worked daily with technical materials at the Knoll's Atomic Power plant and at the General Electric facility were interested in reading them more quickly, but I had to disappoint these engineers for the intense program worked best with fictional and non-fictional works. They did benefit from the course, but it may not have met their expectations.

My job was multi-faceted and, fortunately, I was autonomous. I ordered instructional materials, attended conferences, communicated with parents, and visited local high schools to obtain new ideas and to determine the quality of my programs. I also completed federal reports, worked with the entire faculty on individual student's reading problems or with any department that wished to create alternative textbooks or materials for students with lower readability levels.

For example, a social studies teacher and I, through a federal grant, compiled a textbook that was written at a 5th grade reading level. The alternative text, even though it was at a lower readability level, still had to cover the topics outlined by the 9th grade social studies syllabus.

The social studies teacher used the revamped textbook with students who had difficulty working with the regular 9th grade textbook which was actually written for college level students. It had not occurred to the Social Studies Department that the 9th grade textbook may have been too difficult for the students who had failed or were failing the course.

I was also asked to join the Department Chairmen's group- the heads of the school's educational departments. We made policy and monitored events at the high school level.

I expanded to other areas that were not solely educational.

A biology teacher, who eventually became one of my closest friends, asked me to assist her in leading the NHS Outing Club. As a group, students and interested teachers would, on weekends, climb one or two of the Adirondack High Peaks (there are 46 that are higher than 4,000 ft.), camp in the Adirondack Park, or canoe on a wilderness lake.

Eventually, I took over the club and added officers, meetings and methods of raising money for equipment, such as tents, sleeping bags etc. Students who were drawn to outdoor adventure, but who could not afford the expensive but necessary equipment, could then borrow the equipment from the club.

Niskayuna, like many suburban schools, had about 15 percent of its students representing a segment that had learning disabilities. These were the students whom I primarily taught. Some also congregated in the school's – then legitimate - smoking room. They seemed to have the most behavioral problems.

I believed that it were possible to gather a few dedicated teachers and administrators who would be willing to work to change the students' attitudes. The Impact Committee that I spearheaded had that goal in mind.

The Impact Committee was composed of a librarian, one administrator, a member of the Board of Education, the Guidance Department Chair and teachers who represented all four grades.

As a unit we implemented changes. We began a school-wide birthday calendar where a student's name was mentioned during the morning announcements. The librarian gathered interested students and began to landscape the school's property. A teacher became the advisor of the smoking room and had its occupants highlight the room with their own fantasy-themed mural. We hired a person to oversee the behavior in the room. Another teacher organized these students to raise money for the Christmas Wish

Foundation by having pancake breakfasts and spaghetti dinners. We also published a newsletter that advertised the students' projects and achievements.

The guidance counselor and I managed an Outward Bound program that meshed student leaders with students from the smoking room. We hired professional Adirondack guides, Sharp Swann and Ken from the Willsboro Outdoor Center to lead a weekend winter hike in the Great Range area of the Adirondack Mountains. The guides led us up the icy escarpments of Gothic Mountain in darkness in minus 60 degree weather. We were in search of Haley's Comet.

We used crampons on the ice and had to pull ourselves up using the iron cables that were affixed to the steep cliffs to get to the summit of the mountain. We were disappointed, for when our guides located the comet in the horizon, it looked like a burnt, baked potato.

We were exhausted by the end of our trip. Two of the participants came down with the flu and I inherited a frost-bitten knee.

The lesson that the adults learned from the Outward Bound trip was that the smoking room students were better able to handle the challenges that the trip provided: it was bitter cold, the climb was extremely strenuous and students were not allowed to smoke.

By the end of the three day adventure, the smoking room contingent most often reached out to help other students or adults. They were the first to offer a helping hand to jump a frozen stream or to close a strap on a snowshoe. The students who were the leaders in the school environment were only too glad to accept help from someone they might have originally ignored. From my perspective, it was a very successful venture.

Chapter 35

"My name is Maria Beurmann"

I experienced only two problems at NHS in the 14-year span of time that I taught there. The school was noted for its scholarship and achievements, so hubris, or pride, may have caused some individuals to take liberties.

I went to the teacher's lounge during a lunch period to be among adults, but it was not with the intent to socialize. I randomly sat next to a social studies teacher who was known for his dramatic and outlandish behavior. For example, he would walk into a classroom while the teacher was lecturing and burst into an operatic song. At times, he would pursue a student down the hall calling out comments. It was unclear as to why the school allowed such unprofessional behavior, but that was part of the charm of NHS – it attracted artistic and creative personnel.

He must have had an argument in the morning with his wife because he was in a foul mood when I sat next to him. (I was told later that I somehow reminded him of his wife and that was the reason for his behavior on that day).

As I was eating my lunch, the teacher placed his hand on my thigh and began stroking it. He then took his french fries, pushed them in and out of his mouth and said "I could really show you how to eat these."

I had been told by teachers in other school systems that I was conservative in my demeanor, so I was unsure why he was coming on to me, especially since I had not spoken to him.

I had worked with the man within an educational context, but had never partied and had rarely spoken with him. He was too much of a stage performer for my taste.

I was disgusted by his behavior.

I got up during his pantomime with the french fries, left the lounge and headed toward the main office. When I entered the office I lost my composure.

The secretary to the principal was a friend who listened to my tearful tale. I had had it with the bombastic teacher and decided to follow through so to curtail, what I believed, was unacceptable behavior.

I contacted the teacher's union representative and the Commission on Human Rights. Their representative advised me to sue the teacher and the school; however, the school system had treated me well and I did not want its reputation tainted.

I asked the principal, the vice principal, the teacher and the union representative to meet with me in the principal's office. I told them my findings and the Commission's recommendation to bring a civil and a criminal suit against the teacher and the school. I then read a letter that I had written for the occasion that informed the teacher that I wanted no contact with him except in an educational situation. My final statement to him was,

"You are without honor!"

All this had transpired toward the end of the school year, so I believed that the summer vacation would conceal the entire situation; however, I received a call from the superintended of our school district. He invited me to lunch and he broached the incident.

He told me that when he had spoken to my principal, the superintendent had said of the teacher,

"He picked the wrong person" …to harass.

Women teachers and parents of female students called me during the summer to thank me for interceding. The teacher had a history of harassing young female teachers and older female students.

The friend who had asked me to become the advisor of the Outing Club was the vice president of the League of Women Voters. She relayed my situation to the members of the group. Ironically, the teacher was running for a political office in the Saratoga Springs area. When the story spread, he lost the election.

When school began in September, his behavior was radically different. He was very quiet and kept to himself during our first faculty meeting. It was evident that the repercussions of his actions were being felt.

The second incident involved an administrator. He was lonely and was interested in me; he kept subtly pressuring me for a date. I kept politely putting him off since he was older and not my type. When it became an issue of appropriate body distance, I knew that I would have to take more drastic measures to demonstrate my lack of interest.

He had asked me to a musical affair at Proctor's Theater; dinner and an operatic performance. To get my message across, I dressed down. I wore a wool checked hunter's jacket, heavy wool pants, wool socks and Vibram–soled hiking boots. I even wore a red kerchief around my neck. I looked exactly like I did when hiking in the Adirondack Mountains.

He was gracious enough not to wince when I opened my front door to greet him. He graciously offered his arm to escort me to his car.

Before and after the dinner and the performance, he introduced me to his friends. They all demonstrated class; no one commented on my outfit, or asked if I had taken a shortcut from the trails.

I never again was asked to attend an affair with him. His manner remained professional and he maintained the distance I required. Since no one ever referred to the incident, he proved to be discrete and a gentleman.

Chapter 36

"My name is Maria Beurmann"

I had two serious relationships while teaching at NHS. One gentleman deserved the nickname "Buccaneer" while the other was truly a Rhodes Scholar.

The Buccaneer and I were involved in behind-the-scenes adventures. He looked and acted like a swashbuckling pirate. He selected the most beautiful women in the school to date and even courted some of the most talented students that I have ever met.

We were not officially dating, but I joined him in escapades. We once were accidentally locked in a building during a school-wide overnight conference. We were not able to find a door that was unlocked so that we could leave the building. So that none of our peers would find us in the morning in a no-trespassing area, we spent the night under a baby grand piano. Surprisingly, no one missed us.

I had a more cerebral relationship with the Rhodes Scholar. We had similar backgrounds, in the sense that they were traumatic. His father was an alcoholic who would blunt my friend's boyhood spirit by chaining him for hours to a tree.

He and I ventured to complete the Fulton Chain of Lakes in the Adirondacks. With his background as a soldier in the Korean War, we both felt safe enough to confront both man and beast.

The Fulton Chain is part of the 740 mile Northern Forest Canoe Trail that begins at Old Forge, New York and ends in Maine. Our intent was to begin at Old Forge at First Lake, work through the next seven lakes and end at Middle Saranac Lake. We intended to take six to seven days to complete the 120 miles.

I had not been forewarned by my partner that camping was not one of his favorite pursuits. I found out later that while serving in Korea he had lost his patrol bivouacking. His men had the misfortune to be run over by American tanks while they were sleeping.

Our trip started with an argument over a rope. I proposed that we needed rope because it could be used to stabilize a tent, to drag our canoe over a shallow stream bed or to hoist bags of food in a tree away from a bear's eager paws. My friend believed that it was useless to carry the extra weight.

We loaded our equipment in the canoe, traveled through the eight lakes, dragged our canoe through connecting streams and reached our first sign of trouble.

We were on Raquette River and had decided to stop for the night when we found a lean-to along the river bank.

We unloaded our gear and dumped it into the lean-to. When we began to inspect the perimeter of our campsite, I immediately noticed the empty food containers near the lean-to. I told my friend that we might have a problem with animals since people were using the surrounding area as a dump site.

We fixed dinner, changed our clothes that smelled of the food that we had cooked for our supper and hung up our bags of provisions 15 feet high and 10 feet away from the trunk of a tree. While we were waiting for evening to descend, we could hear people at the neighboring lean-tos. The lean-tos were each about a quarter of a mile away from ours, but they were not visible because of the dense growth of trees and shrubs.

The topic of bears had been raised while we were waiting for the night to settle in and we discussed possible responses to a bear attack. I had suggested that we move to opposite corners of the lean-to, shine our flashlights in the bear's eyes and tell the creature(s) to go away. We still had our backpacks in the lean-to, but had emptied them of all lotions, toothpaste or foods. We were ready!

We both fell asleep. I slept near the edge of the lean-to while my friend backed me. It had to have been about ten o'clock at night when I was awakened by gunfire and shouting. I whispered,

"Bears."

The panicked confusion lasted for a short period of time and quiet once more descended.

Some time passed, but this time our sleep was interrupted by frenzied yells and the sound of someone hitting pots and pans together. Again, after a short period of time, only the sound of the rushing river could be heard.

It was about 4:00 in the morning when I was awakened by snuffling noises. My view of the stars was blotted out by a huge bulk. I jabbed my friends' torso so to wake him. We moved into the corners of the lean-to, turned on our flashlights and shone the beams in the bear's eyes. The bear stopped his climb, turned toward the river and lumbered away.

I had noticed that the bear had been heading toward my friend's backpack, so we moved the empty packs to the river bank and propped them against the trees.

Around 5:00 o'clock in the morning, when the light holds a pearly luminescence, two heavy bulks reared up from the river. Both bears headed toward our backpacks.

One of the beasts picked up a backpack with its paws, hefted it into the air and with a mighty swipe of its claws tore it into ribbons. It mauled the backpack for a few minutes and moved back toward the water. The second bear woofed and soon followed his partner.

We did not move a muscle or utter a sound. My blood was rushing to my head so hard that it felt like a drumbeat. My body jerked on the wooden floor in time with the pounding of my heart.

I couldn't fathom why the bear attacked my friend's pack but not mine. When we gained the courage to step from the protection of the three walls, we pulled apart his backpack. His rain gear was completely tattered and rendered useless. The rain cover and his pack was mangled and covered with black slime, but we did discover, at the bottom of the pack, what had driven the bears to go berserk - one bag of Orange Pekoe Tea. The scent of the tea had driven the bears to totally destroy my friend's gear.

We were exhausted but waited until we reached an island before we sank into a deep sleep. After a day and a night's rest, we continued on our watery journey and completed our 120 miles of canoeing in six days. We didn't have any more confrontations with bears.

Unfortunately, our eight-year relationship did not survive the trauma of the trip.

As a footnote. Between the teaching positions at NHS and my job with NYS Division for Youth I held a job as a Security Supervisor at Albany's International Airport. I was amazed one day to see the tall form of the Buccaneer moving through the security gate. The humor that was always present between us had not abated. He had married, obtained another degree and became a Superintendent of Schools in the NYC area. It was enjoyable reminiscing about our time at NHS, but we both had established different lives, so we moved on.

There is a circle of life.

Chapter 37

"My name is Maria Beurmann"

I was free.

My marriage ended quickly and quietly, just as T.S. Elliot wrote in one of his works, "Not with a bang, but with a whimper."

I was in my early 30's when Jay and I divorced. Jay had joined the army and was stationed in Korea. Julia stayed with him whenever and wherever possible during her summer vacations and I was free to roam. My gypsy spirit resurfaced as I began to travel during the summer months.

William Shakespeare had become my favorite playwright during college. A fellow English teacher, who had worked with me in Averill Park, agreed to join me on a trip to Stratford-on-Avon, England to view some of "The Bards" more popular plays.

Our visit to the island "across the pond" was interesting. During the day, Sue and I would walk in Hyde Park to listen to citizens voicing their complaints in the Speaker's Corner. We would visit the local tourist sites or attend a play. It was a culture shock to see how an English audience reacted to an American play, such as "Hair," and how Americans would sit stone-faced during an English play while the locals roared in appreciation. We realized that an audience has to be aware of the cultural and physical aspects of a country to find humor or meaning in a play, book or song.

The weather was consistent. It didn't matter whether we were out day or night; it rained. We huddled, eight out of the nine days of the trip, under black umbrellas while in London or as we traveled by rail to other parts of England or Holland.

At night, we journeyed the subway from station to station checking out different night spots. Victoria Station was one of my favorite stops since it was where I had my first taste of pasties, or meat-filled pies. I also enjoyed kidney pies, but found most English food rather bland.

A mistake we made before we went partying throughout London was that we did not know the difference between English bars and English nightclubs. Locals tended to go to bars rather than nightclubs because, as we were told afterwards, the nightclubs were controlled by different factions, or mobs.

In the nightclubs, everyone was dressed to the nines – another fact that we were not aware of. Since we were unaware of the mores, we dressed in business casual. The stylishly dressed Turkish crowd identified us immediately as foreigners from our clothes. Two men disengaged themselves from their cadre of followers to draw us into a conversation. We did not know that the group frequenting the nightclub that evening was equivalent to the Turkish mob. In our ignorance we were very open with our backgrounds and our trip to England.

The leader of the group, Vince, took an interest in me and assigned himself as my protector for the entire evening. He called a man over to attend to Sue, but he turned out to be very young; perhaps 17 or 18 years old. Sue was in her early 30's. Vince did not give Sue any choice in the matter; the young man became her evening companion.

I had a night of interesting conversations and sights, for there was a mixture of many nationalities and a Babel of languages intermingling in the club. As it neared midnight, I told Vince that we needed to hire a taxi to take us to our hotel. He mentioned that the taxis stopped running at 11:00 p.m.

We had no means of transportation, so when Vince offered us a ride to the hotel in his limousine we accepted his invitation.

Both men escorted us into our hotel and then walked us to our room. When Sue opened the door, Vincent shouldered his way into the room. Sue's escort grabbed her, threw her on the bed and jumped on top of her. When he began to fondle her, I told both of them that they had to leave, or I was going to start screaming for help. I could tell by the young man's reaction that Vince made a derogatory remark about us in a foreign language, but after they laughed, they left. Thankfully, we did not encounter any more unusual situations, but we did not frequent any more clubs.

Later in the week; however, I experienced an event much like that illustrated in Ernest Hemmingway's novel, For Whom The Bells Toll.

I have always been piqued by the statement that the earth moves when a person meets another individual with whom there is an instant simpatico. The shifting of the earth may happen at the first glance or when making love.

Sue and I had entered a restaurant to order lunch. The tables were completely full, but as I looked for a seat I met a younger man's glance. I felt the electric charge between us as he beckoned to me and patted the seat next to him. I sat and Sue slid next to his friend.

We exchanged pleasantries as we waited for our meal. Evan lived in Barbados and was on a holiday in England. By the end of the meal, he had invited me to visit his home for a week or two.

I was astounded by the immediate, mutual attraction. I had trouble focusing on anything but him. I found myself taking shallow breaths, and I immediately began to make plans to visit Barbados. The four of us were inseparable for the next few days.

.

Chapter 38

"My name is Maria Beurmann"

At home, I paid bills, caught up with house and yard work, and then packed summer clothes for my trip to Barbados. As the cruise ship moved toward the dock in Barbados, a steel band and hordes of natives greeted us. I disembarked in the midst of heat, dust and poverty. Evan was there to greet me and to set things in motion.

My host took me to his home, a gated community that was surrounded by high, black fencing. On the way there, I noticed that the majority of the population was black. We seemed to be the only white people on the rough and dusty road.

When the gates of the estate opened, a crowd was gathered in the courtyard. It seemed that a celebration was in the works, but I sensed it was not for my arrival. All of the celebrants, except for the wait staff, were white. Evan explained that the ruling class, which he and his parents were part of, represented 5% of the population while the black people who lived outside the compound represented the remaining 95%.

Evan had tasks to complete during the day in the compound, so I took advantage of the sun and the public beaches that were open to tourists, but my attempts at leisure had unexpected results. Because the general population was poor, they tended to closely track the tourists to beg for money or goods. On one occasion, I had to run through the Kentucky Fried Chicken restaurant to escape a man who had been following me to beg for money.

I wasn't the only tourist experiencing problems with the locals. One of the tenants in my motel was robbed. The thief had climbed on the roof of the building and had swung on a rope to get into the building. He crashed through the balcony door to get into the man's room. The tenant's jewelry and money were stolen, but the police were not able to find the thief or help the tourist gain back his property.

When Evan had free time, he and I cruised on his motor bike around the perimeter of the twenty mile island.

The scenes that I viewed were testament to the poverty of the island; naked children scrabbled in the dirt, a Mass was being conducted by a priest in full religious raiment. He administered Holy Communion to his two parishioners as they stood in the midst of clucking chickens that pecked at the dirt. Their weather-beaten hovel was the size of an outhouse.

When I was in my early 30's, my daily exercise was to run a couple of miles every morning. On my first morning in Barbados, I woke up at 5:00 a.m. prepared to run on the narrow, dirt road that fronted my motel. I was shocked to see the entire community awake and patiently waiting on the curb. I was unnerved by the sight of an unending line of black people staring at a white woman running by. I had the courage to only run that morning. Their poverty and apathy was so obvious that my run appeared to me as a foreign and frivolous pursuit. The men, women and children seemed to have nothing to do and nowhere to go.

That year's crop – cane sugar – had failed because of adverse weather conditions. The villagers had to resort to gathering the next cash crop – blowfish –that when emptied could be used as decoration, lamps and night lights.

When I commented on the abject poverty of the
island and the contrast between the two classes, Evan
admitted that the natives were becoming more aggressive
and restless because of the looming shortages and the lack of
money and goods.

It was enlightening to see the dichotomy that existed
between the two classes, the acceptance of the disparity and
the stilted interactions between the two groups of people.

At night, Evan and I joined his friends at the beach
that surrounded his home. We spoke for hours comparing
life on the island to life in the US mainland. If we were not
enjoying the bonfires at the beach, we attended parties at the
compound.

Money was a bit tight because this was my second trip
during my summer vacation, so I initially made the attempt
to cook meals at the motel, but when I shopped at the local
grocery store either there was very little food available on the
shelves, or the meat and produce were unrecognizable.

Since "When in Rome, do what the Romans do," I did
chance buying a few products from the store, such as a
package of meat and some shriveled vegetables, to cook at
my motel room. When I sniffed and kneaded the meat, it was
not beef, pork, or chicken. The texture was grainy and

marbled with fat and the taste was unrecognizable. I couldn't force myself to try it or to give it away, that's how much I was repelled by its smell and texture.

I asked Evan what type of meat was imported to Barbados, but since he did not do the shopping or involve himself in the cooking of food, he couldn't provide any information. For all I know, I might have bought kangaroo meat from Australia or a local cat. I ate very little of the local food, but instead depended on eating my main meals at the compound with Evan. In my motel room, I subsisted on crackers, cookies, juice and candy.

The week's visit was a unique experience. Evan's family graciously treated me as his guest and friend. They made me feel welcomed. Since he was several years younger than I, the parents may have believed that I was a foreign cougar lusting after their son. I'm sure he did not share how we met in England, and that I was an English teacher. His friends, however, knew some of my background, and because I expressly had come to Barbados to be with Evan, they assumed that I must be rich. His friends readily accepted me: I was white, a teacher, wealthy and naturally was in the same social strata as their parents who were part of the compound community.

I had not realized how much younger Evan was until I overheard his conversations with his friends. Their goals were not wholly realistic since they lacked the patina of experience and had not yet ventured off their island, but for me it was another adventure. I treated it as a summer romance.

I still fondly remember Evan, the soft, summer nights and the profusion of fragrant, exotic flowers that enveloped the compound.

Chapter 39

"My name is Maria Beurmann"

I have followed the guiding principle of Bashido, or the Samurai's "Way of the Warrior" since I was in my 30's. I became a practitioner of the Okinawan style of martial arts when I was 36 years old and was a black belt karate instructor for over 30 years.

When my daughter was 16 years old, she attracted the notice of a local boy who was befriended by my ultra-religious neighbors. In an attempt to entice Julia, the teen filled my mailbox with burnt cigarettes, deflated my car's tires, broke part of our front screen door, stalked the perimeter of our home on winter nights and was generally a major nuisance in the neighborhood. When I contacted the New York State Troopers to place him on their watch list, because of his misadventures, they informed me that they were unable to intervene unless he physically hurt my daughter or me.

The juvenile delinquent became dangerous. He escalated to setting fires in people's backyards. He harassed several of his older neighbors by calling them at all hours of the night. He wrote his adopted sisters' phone numbers on bathroom stalls. He eventually was placed in jail when he struck a little girl because she refused to give him her seat on the school bus. The neighbors, who felt compassion for him because of his personal problems, allowed him to perch on their front porch where he could smoke, throw cigarette butts on the ground and keep track of our comings and goings.

To combat my feelings of helplessness and to protect my daughter, I joined a karate school or dojo. I am now retired from the sport, but I believe that the Okinawan style of karate greatly impacted my life. It gave me strength, confidence and practical self-defense skills.

It took 30 years of hard work, commitment and exercise to achieve a 7th degree black belt, or a 7th Dan. I have taught numerous individuals and groups of all ages and abilities katas (martial arts dances), kumite (fighting skills), how to use weapons and how to defend themselves against punches, kicks, knives, or guns.

I have never had to use the killing techniques that are taught in the martial arts. The best advice that I offered our students over the years was to use their intelligence to determine the level of danger. If it were a choice between life or death, then they were to use the most basic and lethal of techniques as quickly as possible and then run away. It's a simple theory; it's better to be safe than sorry.

I had many opportunities to showcase my skills. I competed over the years in both katas and fighting throughout New York State. I learned some judo, tai chi, a little Aikido and the use of a war fan. My main instructor, who was also the owner of the karate studio, awarded me the various ranks as I learned the necessary requirements to advance in the Okinawan style.

My Sensei (head instructor) would receive requests from schools, businesses, television stations, women's groups, rape crisis centers and once or twice other martial arts studios to demonstrate or to teach skills in which our instructors excelled. After I taught or performed, all I asked as payment was a small plaque as a record of the community service which I completed. Sensei would hang the plaques in the studio.

Compared to other karate dojos in the tri-city area, our studio was unique because we formulated an instructional textbook or manual of our style to give to our instructors and our students as a guide.

Creating an instructional manual was an arduous task that required quite a bit of patience and time. Six high-ranking instructors met every Saturday for three years to review what each instructor had written during the week. He or she had the choice of selecting a skill (such as a response to an over-head knife attack) that piqued his or her interest. We began at the basic, white belt level skills and when these were written, proofread and performed we moved to the next level and its skills. Eventually, we reached the black belt levels and repeated the same process to ensure that the instruction was standardized and understood by both instructors and students.

The ranks in our dojo began with the white, advanced to blue, orange, green, purple, three levels of brown and ten levels of black. The Master level was granted when an individual moved beyond the 5th Dan, or a 5th degree black belt instructor..

The explanation or description of the skill had to be clearly written so that parents and students could easily understand the attacks and the responses. Because of my background as a reading and English teacher, I was able to transpose the instructors' texts into a 5th grade level script so that it could be grasped by the majority of our students.

It was a slow process. On a Saturday morning, I read the guidelines for each rank to a pair of instructors. They performed the moves. If the moves were not clear to the other three instructors and our Sensei, then the directions were rewritten and performed again by the same martial artists. The final result of all that effort was a standardized set of instructions, or a manual that the practitioners of our Okinawan style of karate could use to teach students.

Competitions, where katas and fighting skills were judged by instructors from various martial arts styles, were an integral part of becoming a well-rounded martial artist. By competing, a student could judge himself or herself against martial artists from other schools.

I competed statewide in both katas and fighting and brought home several first place wins, especially in fighting. From 36 to 45 years of age, I often fought women in their 20's. It was common to have both genders compete against each other when doing katas but, when fighting, men were placed against men and women fought women of similar rank. My last competition was when I was in my 40's. My competitor was a woman in her 20's who had qualified for the Olympics. I placed second in that match and finished with a cracked eyebrow ridge and a displaced contact lens.

When I began karate, I was an oddity for I was older and was well educated. I became a role model when I began to compete and win at the competitions. Because I was aggressive and was quite confident of my karate skills, I was approached by female students. They asked if I were interested in dating them, but I would just say,

"It's not my thing."

The young women took the rejections gracefully, especially since I didn't make an issue of the invitations and because, by then, I was an established, high-ranking karateka (karate student) and instructor.

I was a fighter and was seen, or so I was told, as formidable. That might have caused students to ignore the taboo of an instructor/student relationship. Our Sensei; however, did not tolerate any interrelationships between instructors and students, even though it did occasionally occur. As the first woman instructor in our school and as an aggressive martial artist, I was too unique and too much in the limelight to be approached by any male student who might have considered a relationship. I was; however, in several relationships with other karate instructors.

My greatest satisfaction came from seeing students gain confidence and skills to reach their goal: advancing through the rainbow ranks toward the coveted black belts. By the time an individual reached the 10th Dan, karate had become a lifetime sport.

My rallying motto for my students was "Excellence, Confidence and Respect." The students who were committed and possessed the necessary "fire in the belly" excelled and achieved their goal.

If a student wished to aim for the "Dan" (the ranks in the black belt levels) he or she had to promote the sport throughout the community. For example, a martial artist could engage in the community's "Wellness Day," be interviewed on television on the benefits of the sport, teach self-defense classes in local schools, or conduct seminars on weapons, such as car keys, combs, umbrellas, canes etc., that could be used in everyday situations. The more practical the demonstration or seminar, the more attractive it was to the general public.

As a student, I benefited from working with various high-ranked instructors. I also gained a more comprehensive knowledge in the martial arts by taking classes in different styles, such as judo or aikido. I took from each style and teacher what worked for me and learned to respect the sport, the instructor's knowledge and his or her skills.

Even though I retired after 30 some years of performing and teaching, I still perceive myself as a student, because a person never stops learning. The principles behind the martial arts served and continue to serve as a guidebook for much of my life.

Chapter 40

"My name is Maria Beurmann"

I was keeping busy between raising Julia, teaching high school, teaching karate and traveling in the summers, but something was still missing. I desired friends who shared similar interests.

I began to volunteer as a reading teacher at an alternate prison in Troy for a couple of hours a week. The man who ran the educational programs, Pat, belonged to an encounter group that was composed of professional people in their 30's; a lawyer, two teachers, a married couple and an architect. Pat, who was doing the volunteering as pro bono work, lived with his partner, the architect.

Pat and I decided to introduce some of the agency's prisoners to camping and canoeing at one of my favorite lakes in the Adirondack Preserve; Forked Lake. The prisoners, who were in their late 20's, had rarely traveled from their urban homes. The idea of roughing it in the wilderness must have been terrifying. Of course, they would never have admitted to such a lame emotion.

Pat and I enjoyed taking risks and attempting new ventures. We had bought a kayak kit and had spent innumerable hours constructing it. We decided to test its sea-worthiness on a remote Adirondack lake and some nearby streams. The boat proved to be exceedingly light, but the leather body and wooden frame seemed rather flimsy; however, it did float and it did carry both of us without tipping over.

An Adirondack Stream

Swiftly the current flows,
Bearing us into raging torrents.

Foam flecked,
Swollen by nightly storms.

Tossing our craft
Like a leaf in autumn winds.

We used the kayak several times during the summer, but I didn't see him using it the following summer, so he might not have had much faith in its sturdiness.

The prisoners were apprehensive of the handmade boat, the rental canoes and the camping site that was on an island. As Pat and I cooked dinner over the campfire they crowded around us amazed by our quiet efficiency with primitive gear. They tried to act "cool" and unconcerned when the night descended and they had to head for their sleeping bags in their tents, but the raised voices that fluctuated during the night were testimony to their nervousness. It was their first experience with the nocturnal sounds of loons and of the Great Canadian Horned owls. I believe that they underwent an attitude adjustment by canoeing and camping with us. They were ready to pack and jump in the boats when we decided the following morning to head for home.

Chapter 41

"My name is Maria Beurmann"

Pat invited me to join his encounter group. My daughter, Julia, had no choice but to go everywhere with me, for I was extremely strict and protective of her due to my own experiences and background. By now, Jay was living in another state, so he rarely saw her during the school year.

I found solace with these people. We cross-country skied down Gore Mountain, jumped in the frigid waters of Forked Lake in early spring, camped in the Adirondacks and stayed at cabins at SUNY-Albany's remote Dippikill property. The area was so pristine that Julia burst into tears when she saw, for the first time, skies devoid of artificial light. The velvet night was filled with an amazing array of pinpricks of light and shooting stars.

Julia was witness to some adult shenanigans, such as grown adults stripping naked in the middle of winter to pose for a picture on a frozen lake. She and I laughed to see the group shivering and hugging each other to stay warm. In no way was I or Julia tempted to join them in that prank.

She also was privy to group meetings in dim rooms, watching the smoke rise from burning incense or listening to music by James Taylor, Bob Dylan, the Eagles or Carol King while the adults smoked pot.

Julia was also with me when bears invaded our campsite on Forked Lake. The bears were drawn to our camp because we had placed bread and peaches for safe-keeping on the roof of the outhouse. It was bedlam in the middle of the night when the bears knocked down the outhouse, trampled the peaches, ate the entire loaf of whole wheat bread but ignored the inexpensive white bread.

I was tempted to write a testimonial to the company that made the whole wheat bread and state that the bears preferred their bread over the white bread, but I didn't. As they say,

"You had to have been there."

We had some creative geniuses in the encounter group. The architect and the lawyer held some very unusual parties. I recall a Halloween party where the host wore a priest's cassock that was held closed at the neck with one button. He also wore roller skates and strategically placed red, white and blue feathers over his privates. It was worrisome to see this big man flying toward the front door to greet a guest.

Julia and I, of course, wore more conservative costumes. She was in an Indian costume and I had made for myself a long green dress that had red and yellow flowers sprinkled throughout it. I topped the dress with a large, multi-colored crepe-paper hat which represented a spring flower. Since this was the time of the flower children, I dressed as a flower child.

Chapter 42

"My name is Maria Beurmann"

It must be a defect in my character, because when I encounter problems, I internalize them. Before the divorce was finalized, I came down with colitis and was hospitalized for several days. I didn't recognize the illness and neither did the hospital, but the stomach pains, weight loss and the coughed-up blood concerned me. I was placed on intravenous and was told to relax.

During this episode, I learned that a childhood experience can affect an adult even though decades have passed. The colitis was so active that the hospital staff decided not to feed me for a day or two so my stomach could settle down. I slept, but was plagued by nightmares that kept reoccurring the entire night.

I was back in the orphanage. I was starving and the place was under siege. Bombs were shaking the foundation of the building. I was terrified and demoralized.

My screams soon brought a nurse, and to explain my behavior, all I could yell was,

"The bombs! The bombs!"

When I was fully awake, I told her that I was starving and needed food. I must have looked like a depraved and desperate adult for she shortly brought a bowl of stew that consisted of beef, onions, peppers and tomatoes.

For anyone with an intestinal illness, that particular combination of roughage and acidic foods is one of the most lethal of mixtures. I devoured the meal only to vomit it all up on the bed and on the floor. In the distress of the moment, I attempted to climb out of the hospital bed, but then sprawled on the floor and passed out.

When I came to, a new meal of rice, toast, tea and pudding was on the tray. That fare, which was more suitable for stomach problems, calmed me down and helped me to get a couple of hours of dreamless sleep.

Chapter 43

"My name is Maria Beurmann"

When my mother realized that I was beginning to travel extensively, she asked me if I would accompany her on a cross-country trip to California. She had never traveled beyond the Mississippi River and this trip was the answer to a dream.

I gathered my camping equipment, called Triple A for a map and prepared an itinerary for a car trip from Fredonia, New York to California's border.

We drove about 250 miles on the first day and found a campground before nightfall. I cooked a meal over my SVEA camping stove and we settled in for a night's sleep in a four-man, Eureka tent.

It's not comfortable sleeping on a thin pad and a sleeping bag on hard ground. The body reacts negatively to roots and rocks. If it rains, a person has to stay away from the tent's walls, because if contact is made with the walls, water seeps through the cloth onto the sleeping bag or on the person's clothes.

My mother had enough of camping after the first night and volunteered to pay for motels and meals if I would continue to drive and navigate. I took the deal.

We stopped at various hot spots in the national parks and forests, took pictures and admired the views as we traveled through the northern states. We took a side trip to Canada's Alberta Province and returned by crossing the middle states to get back to Fredonia, New York.

I had not expected to confront my mother, but since we were confined to a car for hours at a time, I was able to air some issues that had bothered me since I attended high school. I was abashed when she did not remember the incidents. I had stewed over these slights for years, and I realized when I saw her astonishment, how trivial they were.

We had a pleasant time crossing the United States. She thanked me, but did not dwell on the trip or on the changed relationship between us. She was as reticent as ever.

I believe; however, that my trip with my mother did change the dynamics between us. Her attitude was more accommodating and she seemed to trust me more than she did before the trip. When my daughter asked me to buy a house, rather than living in an apartment, like we had done for most of her life, my mother offered to finance our new home. The offer was sincerely made with no strings attached except to make the monthly payments.

It was extremely generous of her to bankroll the house. She knew that I was having difficulty with the day to day expenses, especially on a teacher's salary. I could not depend on Jay, for he often did not send money for Julia's upkeep.

I made certain to honor the monthly installments, but I was one of the few relatives who ever paid her back. My mother had lent money, in the past, to my adult cousins to build large supermarkets in Orchard Park, New York. She also lent money to local relatives who ran up large bills. Even one of her cousins, a professor in Italy, asked my mother for money.

It saddened me to see how my mother's relations used her. I would travel with her on Sundays to visit relatives who owed her monthly payments. She would attempt to use guilt to motivate them to pay what was due to her. Most of them would change the subject or pay only a pittance of the outstanding principal. Only one cousin, whom I still communicate with, raised the issue of money when my mother passed away. I received the full payment when I acknowledged that I held her promissory note that showed that she owed money to my mother.

My mother was generous, but timid in requesting repayment. I never received any money from any of her other relatives. They all seemed to have disappeared over the years.

It disappointed me to have had them abuse her good nature. Her financial woes served as a lifelong lesson for me, because I have never lent money to a friend or a relative.

Chapter 44

"My name is Maria Beurmann"

My second trip across the United States was with a girl friend and my daughter. It took over 30 days to complete. My friend, Ellen, and I had plans to raft the Colorado River, to ride mules down the Grand Canyon, to climb the Rockies and to shop for jewelry on the Ute and Apache Indian reservations in Colorado and Arizona.

On this trip, we headed north-east toward Michigan's Painted Rocks. We followed the Trans-Canada Highway to the northern Rockies and aimed to return home by traveling through central US so to enjoy other sights, such as the Grand Tetons, Old Faithful and Mammoth Hot Springs in Wyoming and South Dakota's Badlands.

The vistas were amazing in Michigan. I had never seen tides retracting to leave a half a mile of exposed beach and stranded jellyfish. We had to tread carefully to avoid their toxins, the heavy seaweed and the flopping sea life. Sea gulls screeched raucously over a fisherman's catch. Waves boomed and crashed against a rocky shore that afforded a base for a towering lighthouse. I had never seen such a seascape.

As we traveled in Canada, we found the locals, who ran the campsites, surly and antagonistic. They did not welcome us when they spotted our New York license plates. We were targets, however, for the clouds of black flies that hovered in front of our screened tent. Early in our trek through Canada, we learned to rent a campsite for one night and then quickly pack up our equipment in the morning and leave with few regrets.

It was late July as we crested the mountains, but snow still surrounded boulders and filled in low spots when we reached the higher altitudes of Bear Tooth Pass in the Canadian Rockies. We took numerous pictures, threw snowballs at each other, ate lunch among fragrant meadow flowers, and watched the wheeling flight of golden eagles and other birds of prey.

When we finished preparing our site for sleep in a national forest or a national park, Julia and I would sit at a picnic table and we would spend an hour or two reviewing multiplication tables, or computing addition, subtraction and division problems so that she would be better prepared for the upcoming school year. Ellen had the task of cooking our meal and washing the dishes while my daughter and I worked on math.

Julia may not have enjoyed the journey as much as my girl friend and I did. On occasions, when we were at a state park, the park rangers would provide the residents and tourists at the campground nature programs on the local flora and fauna. If the programs were not available or if it rained we would walk the campgrounds in our wet weather gear and greet or talk with other travelers.

Several times, to amuse ourselves, Ellen and I would adjust other people's Eureka tents that had not been correctly assembled. We interfered only if the campers were not at their campsite. It must have been puzzling to the owners of the tents, when they returned to their site, to find the guy-lines tight and the walls and ceiling taut so more headroom was available. Most owners did not read the directions, so the tents usually looked like deflated parachutes before we adjusted them.

As my recommendation to a traveler, it makes sense to purchase a Golden Eagle Pass if traveling cross-country. It is a one time, one price deal, and it provides a family with free admission to any national park, state park or national forest. It is the most economical way to travel if a personal vehicle is used. It's also advisable to ask park rangers for suggestions, for their job is to make travelers feel welcome by providing information and entertainment.

Chapter 45

"My name is Maria Beurmann

Once we reached the border of Vancouver we headed south-east toward the Four Corners area (the nexus of Colorado, Utah, New Mexico and Arizona).

Time Warp

(Arizona)

Follow the mind
To another space and time
Where warriors of old
Spoke of tales untold.

Of savage harmony
Of man and beast,
Of unblemished vitas,

Strident skies,
Thrusting mountains.

Cry for the loss!

We saw miles of limitless prairieland, grazing elk and bison and endless skies. One of the most amazing and frightening sights was to watch a storm gather momentum and sweep toward us with fierce, forked lightning as the harbinger of the storm's ferocity.

Ellen provided the material for an amusing anecdote. We had reached an area in Colorado that is named Red Mountain because of its red soil. This vast area was home to large herds of elk. Ellen decided to pull off the main road because she wanted photos of the grazing animals.

During the trek across Canada and the US, Julia and I became aware of Ellen's mood swings. During these episodes, she would often wander off to be alone. This was one of those times.

She left us and began to follow a herd of elk in the grassland. My daughter and I stayed safely back near the car and waited for her to finish her shots. She was unaware that as she was following the herd, the male elk, or bull, was closely following her. I assumed he was protecting his cows.

Ellen soon crouched down behind a tree to get a closer view of the herd. The bull elk moved closer to her. Julia and I called to Ellen to warn her of the danger, but she became annoyed and waved us away without glancing our way. As she adjusted her body to get a better shot, the bull elk moved right behind her, so that it seemed that he was peering over her shoulder.

Julia and I waved at the elk to distract him, but his total concentration was on Ellen. It must have snorted or made some noise, because Ellen glanced behind her and fixated on the elk's eyes. Her scream caused the bull elk to shake his head, bugle at her and move to rejoin his herd.

Of course, my daughter and I got great pleasure at her distress, since she had made it evident that she did not want our company.

We then traveled to Yellowstone National Park in Wyoming and saw herds of American bison, bighorn sheep and moose, but avoided traveling in areas that were occupied by grizzlies. We had heard stories of a few intrepid souls who ignored the warnings posted throughout the park. They were determined to search out the haunts of these mercurial animals, but in the process were attacked and mauled by the bears. We had little interest in this type of adventure, so we stayed close to our car and other tourists. We also viewed the intermittent spurts of the much sought out geyser – Old Faithful. Yellowstone Park and Yellowstone Lake afforded us distant views of the rugged and majestic Grand Tetons.

I was surprised to learn that Wyoming is the least populated state in our country. You wouldn't have known it by the number of tourists that hogged the roads in Yellowstone National Park.

Chapter 46

"My name is Maria Beurmann

We were closing in on more mountainous terrain in Utah. We depended on Ellen's navigational skills to reach the more scenic sights. I followed her directions, and the scenery and land around us became more desolate and barren.

Eventually, we ran out of paved road and landed in a col where sheep were noisily milling around. All I could see over the hood of the car was the continuing ascent of the mountain, boulders and sheep.

The situation was so absurd that I began to laugh hysterically.

What were we doing in such a wasteland, and can we get out of this predicament?

As Ellen and I were glancing around us, we were surrounded by panicked sheep. The noise of their bleating was overpowering. We did not dare step out of the car to assess the situation, but found ourselves immobilized by the strange situation.

I was trying to rein in my laughter when four horsemen crested the top of the mountain. As in a western flick, they were momentarily outlined by the vast sky. They looked toward our direction and soon trotted down to our car.

Ellen and I became anxious at this point, for we did not know where we were, but the situation was so ludicrous that I continued to laugh as the men stopped in front of our car. They scrutinized our license plates and glanced at our faces with bemused expressions. They had to have thought that we were nitwits sitting on top of a mountain among boulders and sheep. I sheepishly exclaimed "I think that we're lost."

The leader responded with a laconic "Yup!"

I was mortified but I still couldn't stop laughing.

The lead horseman gave me instructions on how to get off the mountain and back to the road. We carefully wended our way among the boulders and sheep, found the rough road and continued our trip toward Colorado.

Chapter 47

"My name is Maria Beurmann

We were able to avert a tragedy while in Colorado. We had driven to Estes Park in the Rocky Mountain National Park system to stay the night. The site we chose for our tent was on the side of a steep hill. Before we settled in for the night, we splurged on a meal at a local Mexican restaurant. Ellen selected a highly seasoned dish and, since Julia and I were not as familiar with Mexican food, we ordered more traditional dishes, such as hamburgers and fries. We did not discover until we returned to our campsite that Ellen's side dish of guacamole was tainted.

It began to rain heavily, so Julia decided to sleep in the car's back seat. She had gotten soaked the last time that she had slept in the tent. With three of us in the tent it tended to get crowded and invariably one of us was forced into the tent's wall as we tossed and turned in our limited space. Osmosis had forced the heavy rain to seep through the wall onto Julia's sleeping gear and clothing.

Ellen and I chose to sleep in the comfort of the tent but, unfortunately, Ellen was hit with Montezuma's Revenge. She was in and out of the tent during the entire night. I became accustomed to hearing the sound of the tent's zipper opening and closing.

When I rose the next morning, it was still raining. The side of the tent that faced the hill was caved in and inundated with water. Ellen felt better, so we quickly struck camp, loaded the wet tent and clothes in the trunk of the car and continued on our trip toward Mesa Verde. We later heard from a park ranger that Estes Park had been inundated with a flood soon after we left. Unfortunately, over a hundred people had drowned. We were grateful to have avoided that natural disaster.

We soon arrived at the Mesa Verde National Park and followed other tourists who were touring the cliff dwellings. We viewed the ancient native dwellings of Puebloans, or Anasazi Indians. Most of the cliff dwellings were devoted to residential or living space, but some of the dwellings had been used for storage or religious rituals. We saw handprints on the plaster walls and faint drawings that were eroded by age. We viewed the kivas – circular, subterranean rooms that were religious in intent. The dwellings were primarily made of adobe bricks that were composed of clay, sand and straw.

The past inhabitants were long gone – over 700 years ago - whether because of the lack of food and water, some natural disaster or violence from neighboring tribes, and they may have migrated to other areas.

It had to have been difficult to subsist on lands devoid of water and fertile soil. It was sad to contemplate the demise of a race.

Chapter 48

"My name is Maria Beurmann

We continued our journey and reached the ancient, striated gorges of the Grand Canyon. We admired and exclaimed over the exposed geologic strata of schist and limestone that was cut by the Colorado River. We rode on horses, since mules were not available, down the unbelievably narrow and circuitous path to the floor of the Grand Canyon. Thankfully, we only saw semi-arid land and did not encounter the ubiquitous snakes. Later that day, we stopped at the lodge on the South rim and had apple pie and hot chocolate.

We had our tent ready for our evening's sleep, but torrential rains made us reconsider leaving the comfort of the lodge, so we huddled around the roaring fire and ordered more hot chocolate. We did not look forward to the walk to our campsite and sleeping in wet gear, but we had no choice since we had not made sleeping arrangements with the lodge. We finally gathered our courage and made our way through the downpour to our tent. Thankfully, we did not encounter any flash floods on the rim of the canyon like those that often decimate the lower reaches.

We also experienced a day-long rafting trip down the Colorado River. Our guides pointed out the vegetation on the higher reaches – pinyon pine and juniper forests - and the different plants on the semi-arid desert floor of the canyon.

It was a tranquil and informative ride and we were able to disembark from the raft to meet and speak with a hermit who lived year-round on the sandy beach by the river. We stretched our legs and used a bush for a "call of nature." Julia seemed to enjoy both the horses and the rafting.

In the evening, after our rafting trip, our guides built a fire and prepared steaks and corn on the cob. We exchanged stories under a vast sky that highlighted the Milky Way. Comets flared and John Denver's song "Rocky Mountain High" was apropos for we did see it "rain fire in the sky".

We finally reached South Dakota's Badlands, its million tributaries, its canyons, and its intense golden sunlight diffusing off of arroyos and orange bluffs.

Our tent was erected under a tree, but near a bluff that plunged into a canyon. The early evening air was pleasant and we were able to eat our supper in comfort.

We had been asleep only an hour when a wind sprang up. Lightning scored the sky and our tent poles began to rattle. When the lightning hit the top of a nearby butte the torched area turned into scoria, or glass. The scoria seemed luminescent in the aftermath of the lightning strike.

We were frightened by the storm for the wind had picked up our tent with the three of us in it and had moved it about a foot closer to the edge of the bluff. In a fit of religious conviction I called out "You and me, God! You and me!"

As we headed toward New York State I was not surprised when the car began to have problems, but I decided to wait until we returned to the Albany area to have it checked out. Many a mechanic imagines a profit when they see tourists having car problems.

I did bring the car to Sears when I returned from our cross-country trip. I explained what we had encountered in

Utah. The salesman gave me an $800 estimate to fix the car. His mistake was that he included a lubrication job in the estimate, but I had lubed the car the night before. At that time, I was more hands-on and I was doing minor tune-ups on my cars myself.

I took the car and the list of repairs that Sears had given me and showed it to the mechanic whom I trusted in Ballston Spa, New York. It turned out that I had bent a tie rod sleeve maneuvering around boulders in Utah. My mechanic quoted a price -twenty dollars to fix the car. That was my proof that some mechanics cannot be trusted when faced with an inexperienced owner and/or a faulty vehicle.

Before taking a long trip, I would suggest that a traveler enroll in a basic car maintenance course. During the cross-country trip, I changed the oil, oil filter, air filter and completed a basic tune-up at least twice. In the long run, I believed it saved me money and trouble.

Chapter 49

"My name is Maria Beurmann"

Toward the end of my 14 year teaching stint at Niskayuna H.S., I received a call from my mother. She was sobbing and saying that she was lost and locked out of her house. Since Fredonia was over 200 miles from my home, I called her neighbor and asked him to use the extra key to allow my mother to enter her home. Soon afterwards, a call came from the Office of the Aging. My mother's neighbors in Fredonia had called the agency because she had been wandering throughout the town dressed in a slip that covered a pair of slacks. The representative's next comment made me extremely nervous. She said

"She has beautiful cut crystal."

I did not see the connection between my mother's possessions and her emerging illness (Alzheimer's). I had noticed that the disease had been affecting her behavior, memory and thinking, but when I had spoken about moving her to my home, I had met resistance from her. The call from the Office of the Aging was a clarion call for immediate action, so I rented a moving van and organized my boyfriend, his sister and her husband to load my mother's possessions on the truck and to immediately move her to the Albany area.

While emptying her rooms, closets and drawers, I found raw chicken covered with maggots, three gold coins and countless newspapers, tattered clothing, decades-old letters and other signs that my mother's illness had advanced. I had hired a woman caretaker to check on her three times a week. She was to cook meals for my mother and to oversee her medications and health. Somehow, even with supervision, things went wrong. Salespeople, from as far as Buffalo, New York, arrived at her doorstep to convince my mother to buy insurance policies. If she had needed to cash the 17 insurance policies, they would have proved worthless since they were duplicated. The insurance representatives had sold her multiple life, auto, house insurances, etc. She never would have been able to collect on any of the policies. To add insult to injury, one of the representatives stole her Social Security checks to cover the cost of his policies.

It's a tragedy that a person, like my mother, who held leadership positions in the community and who was articulate and intelligent, could be diminished by a disease. Mom contracted the type of Alzheimer's that stripped her of speech and mobility. This type was the lesser of two evils. The other type of Alzheimer's, that I have been a witness to, turns a person into a raving, rage-filled lunatic.

For example, one of my mother's neighbors at a Saratoga health facility would smear herself, her bed and the walls of her room every day with her own feces to irritate the director of the adult home.

In NYS, a patient cannot be physically restrained if violent, so the facility's only recourse is to heavily sedate the patient. My mother's illness did not allow her to move, talk or (near the end) swallow food. Even though she was not violent, she still was heavily medicated. Unfortunately, that is the route that most medical facilities follow.

I had been preparing for my mother's move to my area for a year when I had begun to notice her steady decline. I had added a suite to my home for her use. She had her own bathroom, bedroom and sitting room. While she was mobile, she also could use the communal kitchen and living room. She was not able to drive, but had access to my two acres of land, the back deck or could take a daily walk on my street.

Initially, she did visit the neighbors, but her illness made her believe that I had jailed her and had stolen her possessions. I hired friends who monitored her activities while I taught or dealt with appointments.

She lived with me for about two years, but I had to admit defeat; I had absolutely no experience caring for an elderly dementia patient. When my mother lost control of her bladder, my two dogs began to use my house as a bathroom facility. I only had a few choices left.

I resigned from Niskayuna HS. I told my employer that I had reached the point of not recognizing myself when I looked in the mirror.

I reviewed various adult homes and found one about 10 miles away from my home that was situated in the countryside. I visited her every other day for seven years. The owner worked at making the place a home for his tenants, but after years of use, any facility that caters to incontinent adults eventually smells like urine.

The facility could not and would not handle people who became ill or were bedridden, so my mother soon developed a fist-sized bed sore which hospitalized her. When she was cured of the sore, she was placed in a county-run nursing home.

Because my mom was not capable of moving or speaking, she had trouble eating. The staff was not motivated - at an hourly rate of six dollars - to take the time to feed her with a syringe. The medical community is at a loss on how to care for people who cannot explain what ails them, so the elderly are often placed, for hours, in a chair without stimulation and sometimes without care.

Because a nurse's aide usually has to care for six patients per workday, frustration is rampant. Two of my mother's teeth were broken off when a nurse's aide attempted to force the syringe of pureed food into her mouth. Since I was often there at the lunch or dinner hour, I was able to feed her, but it is extremely difficult to deal with patients who have Alzheimer's. Because of the time constraints, some of the patients didn't even get fed.

The 20 years that I monitored my mother's care at various institutions were not pleasant. The clothes that I designed, sewed and washed daily for my mother were often stolen and placed on other Alzheimer's patients who lacked clothes. She, at times, lay in soiled diapers for hours. Her chair, in which she sat for hours, was restricted to the hallway. When I visited my mother, the patients who were lined against the walls of the hallway, would grab my hand and beg for a conversation or a visit.

One would assume that a medical facility would know how to care for an Alzheimer's patient. Within the first month of staying in Saratoga Hospital for an illness, my mother went from 114 to 88 pounds. I was incensed. I requested a meeting with the hospital administration, her doctor and nurses and point blank asked them to justify her weight loss.

They couldn't or wouldn't address my questions.

If I had not been inundated with college classes, my daughter's and my mother's care, I would have sued the hospital. I did inform the group that I was aware that the hospital was in the midst of three other lawsuits.

My mother was returned to the county-run facility. She steadily declined in health and died in 2002. During the 20 years that I monitored her care and her business affairs, I was rightly hyper-vigilant in monitoring her care. When my mother needed hospital care, the hospital would send a doctor to meet me at the entrance. The medical staff knew that I closely supervised their care.

My mother provided me with a life and a future. She served as my mentor and model. To a certain degree, I believe that I paid back my debt to her.

Love you, Mom!

Chapter 50

"My name is Maria Beurmann"

While monitoring my mother's care over the years and supervising my daughter and her growing independence, I continued to search and mingle with people who shared my values - who were fun and not stultifying. I joined the Adirondack Mountain Club and affiliated with the Schenectady Chapter. A friend, who was the Chair of the Schenectady Chapter, asked me if I were interested in becoming the Membership Chair.

I served as the Membership Chair for 32 years.

The main goal or mission of the Adirondack Mountain Club was and is to enjoy and protect the Adirondack and Catskill Forest Preserves. A side benefit of joining the club might be, for some outdoor-oriented people, to climb the 46 highest mountains in the Adirondack Park. All of the high peaks are over 4,000 ft. high.

I spent from 1977 to 1992 questing for the coveted ADK 46'r patch that proved that I had successfully summited all 46 of the highest peaks. Colden Mountain was my first mountain and my 46th was Haystack. I climbed many of the high peaks more than once. I enjoyed climbing the peaks during the summer and autumn months, but about a third of the mountains I summited were completed during the demanding and arduous winter months.

Adirondack Hike

Fog fills mountain valleys,
Highlighted by verdant ranges.

Our steps are
Muffled by gray dampness.

Glimpses of my companions…
Ghosts in the diffused light.

Straying wisps swirl
To reveal distant hills,
Flagged black spruce
That mark the prevailing winds.

We inch upward
Like primordial life forms
Seeking the flare of the morning sun.

I had one friend who was adventuresome enough to accompany me in climbing the more extreme of the 46'rs. She was eager to join me in climbing my final and my 46th high peak - Haystack.

While on the trail to Haystack we came across three people who were doing their annual trek to Marcy. They asked to join us on our way up Haystack and since it is safer to have more than two people on a hike, we welcomed their company.

It was an overcast day when we set out to climb Haystack Mountain. The clouds obscured Haystack and the tops of the surrounding mountains.

It's a tradition to bring wine, champagne or something to drink to toast the end of the quest to climb the 46 highest peaks. We had party favors and a bottle of wine in my backpack that was safely wrapped in a towel.

At the top of Haystack, we opened the wine, put on party hats and began to blow on our noise-makers. We toasted my achievement and took pictures of the event.

Suddenly, a voice resonated through the thick clouds and said "Do you really think you are on Haystack?" We were quite startled, for we were in a whiteout and no one was in sight.

I looked up and asked, "God?"

No one answered my query. We looked at our trail map and realized that we were not on Haystack, but on its neighbor, Little Haystack. We gathered our things, put on our daypacks and headed down the col between Little Haystack and Haystack. Unfortunately, when we reached the top of Haystack, we had no drinks to toast our success, but we did blow on our noise-makers.

On the way back, we saw no one and never knew if we had had divine intervention.

My number as a Forty-Sixer is 3,136. In total, the Adirondack 46r's Club may now have over 8,000 hikers who have earned the much sought-after patch.

Some of my climbs were completed with the Adirondack Mountain Club. Many were hiked with friends, some were done with the Niskayuna's Outing Club and 14 were with my daughter, Julia. I made certain to hike some of my favorite mountains several times.

My favorite was, surprisingly, Allen Mt. at 4,340 feet. It took longer to get to its base, but it has rough escarpments that act like giant steps. It is rugged, wild and challenging.

It's surprising that more deaths or injuries have not occurred in the high peaks. They can be treacherous and if a person is not experienced, or prepared with proper equipment, water and nourishment, they can be deadly. Unfortunately, many of today's hikers heavily rely on the cell phone to get them out of a bind of their own making. They expect assistance from forest rangers or volunteer rescuers when they did not effectively prepare for their hike in the wilderness. There have been recorded deaths, but they are usually not advertised to the general public.

Chapter 51

"My name is Maria Beurmann"

For me, the most difficult of all the peaks to ascend was the Santanoni Range which consists of Panther, Santanoni and the Couchsachraga Peaks. The one time I climbed all three peaks was rough. The leader was inexperienced in leading groups, it rained torrents, the trails were washed out and the leader's goal was an anathema to me; to complete all three peaks as quickly as possible.

Perspective

The glimmer of a mountain lake
Reminder of hiking highs;
When enthusiasm and muscles were new
And people non-existent or few.

When mountain paths were narrow and shallow
And hikers were attentive and mellow.

When litter was an anomaly
And pure water was a reality.

Such irony…
Nostalgic times for a veteran hiker,
But exciting ventures for a novice.

The group was of mixed skill levels and ages. The leader had not checked if the participants had the proper equipment, or if they were able to physically complete a two to three day, arduous trip, so some problems did surface.

One hiker wore jeans, which is not advisable on a hike. Denim cloth offers no insulation, and when wet actually robs heat from the wearer. It is one of the easiest ways to get hypothermia.

A noted retired NYS park ranger, Peter Fish, would always greet hikers entering the high peaks area at Heart Lake with the statement,

"The best dressed corpse in the Adirondacks is dressed in denim."

Our young leader had invited two of his friends, who were completing a forestry program in an Adirondack college, to assist in leading the group. They were interested in applying some of the theories that they had learned in their classes, but their goal was not to lead the hike.

It was raining heavily and the eroded trails were muddy. We had climbed one of the peaks the first day, but we came across another group of hikers who were short of food and equipment. Our three "leaders" left our group to minister to one of the climbers in the other group. We were left alone for an hour or two and I had to deal with one of the older hikers when her boot became stuck in a spruce hole.

When our leaders returned, we continued our hike. Our pace began to increase as the second and third peaks were gained. On the way down the muddy herd path, disaster struck.

My boyfriend and I had complained to the leader that he and his friends were moving too quickly considering the conditions; that the three peaks were trailless and the herd paths had become a muddy morass. The leader ignored our concerns and continued to descend the mountain at a rapid clip.

I neared a declivity and couldn't stop my downward motion in the flowing mud. I fell off a six foot cliff. When I dropped on the ground, I saw the bone in my knee push against the skin and then revert back to its original position. I knew I was going to have difficulty once I stopped, because the pain was already settling in my knee joint.

The group set up camp among the blowdowns, ate a freeze-dried meal and climbed in our sleeping bags. The leader did not approach our tent to check on my condition. I did not get much rest that night since I could not move my leg.

Again, the leader did not approach the group the next morning but stayed with his friends in their tent. He refused our request to speak with him.

Like me, an older gentleman who was part of our group also had had a bad night. He had not brought a rain fly for his tent, so he and all his equipment got drenched. The older woman had worn jeans on the hike and, while packing to leave in the morning, decided to bury her wet jeans in a spruce hole. I forced her to roll up the jeans and carry them in her backpack.

With the above problems and my aching knee, I decided not to depend on our leader and his friends, so I suggested to the remaining hikers that we leave and that we hike the seven miles back to the trailhead by ourselves.

I had been hiking for many years and believed that I was as qualified as our leader. We trekked out in the rain and mud and with the help of walking sticks made it out in good time. It took months of therapy to cure my knee, but eventually I was back on the trails.

Chapter 52

"My name is Maria Beurmann"

Because of one or two frightening events, my daughter is justified in hating anything to do with hiking or camping. After her 14th ascent of the Adirondack High Peaks, she never climbed or camped again.

We were on a Niskayuna Outing Club trip. My friend, who was the original leader of the club, selected a twenty-one mile trip through Indian Pass in the Adirondack Mountains. I felt sorry for Julia, so I volunteered to carry her heavier items, such as her sleeping bag. She only had to carry her extra clothing, her snacks and some community food.

I was additionally burdened with my equipment, my clothing and part of the community gear, such as a tent, food and cooking gear.

It got to a point, during our one day trip, that I dropped on the ground and lay down on my pack to catch my breath. I had never done such an extensive hike and I felt that I couldn't go any further. I think that Julia was just as exhausted, but she may have not wanted to appear weak in front of her peers.

We hiked the entire day, but it took my daughter and I several days to get over that arduous hike.

Another trip that involved the Outing Club may have been the final straw for my daughter. We decided to summit Giant in the Valley - the 11th highest of the High Peaks.

It was autumn in the Albany area and the river valley was wrapped in autumn colors. From past experience, I knew that the upper reaches of the state and the mountains would be barren. The peaks would be smothered in snow and, for certain, some of the mountains would be crusted in ice.

The Myriad Hues of Red

A time of flagrant celebration
Depicted in blushing colors:

The blur of a cardinal's wing
Against shadow-green cedars,

The ruby-red of summer's roses
Heightened by an early frost,

The veins and tips of maple leaves
Leeching into autumn's scarlet,

Evening skies bleeding
Vermilion, pink and sea-green.

A time that flames.
A time that precludes crystal quiet…white cold.

We began the climb to view The Washbowl, and reached a rock face that was covered with a thin sheet of ice. One of the students inadvertently stepped on the ice and began to slide down toward a cliff. As she slid, she grabbed my daughter's leg. Both Julia and my student were now sliding inexorably toward the 100 foot drop.

Thankfully, Julia's boots hit the stone lip at the top of the cliff and their progress was stopped. Both girls were quite shaken, but they had the resolve to continue the 4,627 ft. ascent to the summit. At that time, I didn't dare admit the terror I felt when I saw the two girls seemingly going to their deaths.

Chapter 53

"My name is Maria Beurmann"

As the Membership Chair, I would continue to climb the High Peaks, especially my favorites, but I took on other duties as well.

I was awarded twice with plaques that delineated my achievements and proclaimed me as a Fellow of the Chapter, because I had held the position of Membership Chair of the Schenectady Chapter for so many years.

In the beginning of my tenure as Membership Chair, I satisfied my creative side by designing a pamphlet that described the chapter and its functions. I updated and modernized our monthly newsletter and assisted in compiling a guidebook for trip leaders.

The high school scholarship program began under my tutelage. High School seniors from six local high schools competed for a $500 scholarship to help defray college costs if their degrees were aimed at improving the environment. The only requirement was to write an essay describing their goals and the programs they were pursuing in college. We received many outstanding essays. One of my closest friends now runs this excellent program.

The chapter funded a search and rescue program run by the Department of Environmental Conservation (DEC). I participated in search and rescue sessions and in mountaineering workshops.

One of our search and rescue efforts occurred near the Indian Lake area in the Adirondacks. A hunter, who had heart problems and needed medication to survive, was declared missing by his hunting buddies. He was not properly outfitted with food, warm clothing or medicine when he left his group to explore the area.

The ADK group devised a level 3 search. We created a grid pattern with string and painstakingly walked the area for hours to find the hunter, but it was to no avail. Night was falling, the temperature was plummeting and we had little faith in his ability to stay alive.

Weeks later, a news report mentioned that two young boys found a body near Indian Lake. The body had been half-eaten by coyotes and other animals indigenous to the area.

As the Membership Chair, I also presented, with other board members, seminars on wilderness ethics, equipment, and rules to follow when hiking in the Adirondack or Catskill Preserves. I recommended guide books on summer and winter sports, camping, hiking and canoeing and demonstrated setting up a tent, the best stoves to use, the most comfortable boots and other information that would guarantee the safety of the hiker.

To expand my building skills, I helped to construct, with other ADK members, a lean-to at Silver Lakes on the Northville-Lake Placid Trail. DEC provided the materials and its support. I also assisted in building an extensive wooden bridge at Marcy Dam and poured cement foundations for tents at the Adirondack Lodge at Heart Lake.

Since landscaping is also one of my interests, I helped to design and landscape the gardens at Lake George and at Heart Lake.

All ADK tasks are completed by volunteers who do not ask for monetary reimbursement. Sometimes, the same people may monitor the same lean-to for many years. There are so many trails and so much work to be completed that volunteers can pick and choose if they wish to experience something new. Since the membership is getting older, there is always the need to attract younger people. The jobs; however, can be arduous and some people are not interested in "paying back," or in protecting the mountains for future generations.

Chapter 54

"My name is Maria A. Beurmann"

Because of my many years of hiking and canoeing in the 6.1 million acre Adirondack Preserve, I wrote poetry and photographed many of its extensive lakes, rivers and mountains. I compiled the photos, wrote the poems and published them in two books: <u>Follow The Mind To Another Place and Time</u> and <u>In Celebration…Adirondack Visions</u>. Both feature the beauty and spirit of this preserve that is a mixture of wild and public lands.

The Breath of a Northeaster

A hawk, plump with furled wings,

Settles on a stark branch,
Seemingly content to gaze
At its vast domain.

The lone predator
Views the bleak landscape;
Low, distant hills encompassing
Wide, cinereous waters -
Choppy, foam-flecked,
Eroding the rocky shore.

The wind whistles and
Ruffles the hawk's feathers.
Talons clutch,
Head cocks to smell the sharp nor'easter
Heavy with the hint of ice
And continuous snows.

I presented workshops on writing poetry and used my
books as sources. I also read poetry at schools, writing
expositions, was interviewed by local groups and presented
at bookstores and at televised literary events.

I took my favorite photos, professionally enlarged
them, framed and then displayed them through the Saratoga
Arts Council at libraries, coffee shops, railroad stations,
facilities for the elderly, the Adirondack Mountain Club
headquarters at Lake George and other locations that valued
Adirondack photography. Because of my two published

works, The National Wilderness Society extended an invitation to attend its national annual meeting that was held at Lake George, N.Y. I was to be a part of a panel of notable photographers of the Adirondack Preserve, such as Nathan Farb and Carl Heilman II.

These photographers had more years of experience and have professional equipment that is far superior to mine, but the fact that I was asked to be part of the panel was an honor. I am not as skilled as the other panelists in photography, so I focused instead on reading my poems.

To this day, to promote the creative spirit found in both poetry and photography, I select a middle school or a high school English class and present it with a Christmas gift of a class set of my books to be used as part of their poetry unit.

Chapter 55

"My name is Maria A. Beurmann"

As a martial arts instructor and a teacher of dysfunctional middle school and high school students, I was indirectly connected to law enforcement, since many of the karate instructors in our studio were sheriffs, prison guards or detectives.

I had worked in the Albany school system and in NHS teaching students who had committed minor crimes and who had negative interactions with the law, so when I was offered the opportunity to take classes to become a bodyguard for a local Albany firm, I jumped at the chance. The president of the detective firm provided a 48 hour course on protection detail. His company intended to provide individualized protection for famous performers and sports people, such as Bill Cosby, who were scheduled to present at the Pepsi Arena in Albany, New York or at local theaters and deluxe night spots.

I completed the 48 hour course and received my badge which would allow me access to events, but unfortunately, the Sensei of our karate studio was not willing to pay the exorbitant fees needed to take the remaining 100 hour class. Since that door was closed to me, I applied for a Master's degree at the Rockefeller School of Criminal Justice in Albany.

The degree would provide more occupational opportunities within the criminal justice system, especially since I no longer was teaching; however, I still desired a job that had educational connections and components.

I was accepted at the Rockefeller School that was connected to SUNY-Albany. The Criminal Justice degree program attracted many different occupations: lawyers, guards, policemen and policewomen, truant officers, detectives and the higher echelons of law professionals. I was the only teacher in the program.

The program had two professors who impressed me for two different reasons. One was remarkable in his knowledge of court cases – the judges, the rulings and the rationale behind the rulings, but his interpersonal skills were weak. The second teacher exemplified the traits of a committed educator; he was fair, he listened and thoroughly explained and was open to ideas.

For the first professor, the class had to analyze numerous national and state court cases to determine if the victim was treated *lawfully*. The law does not consider the fairness or unfairness of the case or if the victim was guilty or innocent, but what precedent had been set for that particular case.

His course was mind-boggling. I spent hours trying to determine the rationale of the judges' rulings and why the chief judge ruled for or against the decisions made by the remaining judges. We used reference material to research past cases that supported the final ruling.

The final exam for the course took seven hours to complete, since we were required to analyze 100 court cases to determine if we understood the law. Out of a class of 30 adults, only three or four received an "A." Most of us received average grades. Surprisingly, the law professor had no qualms failing about ¼ to ½ of his students. In a master's degree program, a student is required to earn an "A" or a

"B." "C's" and anything lower were unacceptable and did not count.

As an educator, I was disturbed by the professor's reaction to one young, attractive woman who was a student in his class. I was intrigued by her because her contribution to the entire course was her skill in filing her nails. She never opened a textbook or offered an opinion during class on a case or on a reading. It was obvious that he was very conscious of her presence in his class, for he would direct stories of his out-of-class drinking sessions toward her, but would never address her nail filing.

The second professor spent much of his class time discussing NYS prisons and the life of a prisoner. He also organized trips to prisons that catered to youthful offenders. It was worrisome when he set up a trip to Green Haven Correctional Facility, which is a maximum security adult prison. None of us knew what to expect.

Our instructor advised us to dress down when we visited Green Haven, so I wore my camping clothes and hiking boots. Our professor explained that our intent was to visit the facility, not to turn on the inmates.

We discovered that the prisoners have an efficient system of communication; they had somehow learned that

30 students from SUNY-Albany were coming to visit and to possibly interview some of the inmates.

The prisoners staged a riot to welcome us.

Because of the chaos that ensued, our class was placed in lock-down for several hours. We stared at four walls until we were released for lunch. Because it was also lunchtime for the inmates, they were allowed to traverse the halls to get to the mess hall, so we had no choice but to walk the gauntlet between lines of unshackled prisoners.

We were conspicuous in our dress and our looks since our group was mainly composed of white, middle class individuals. We were also an object of interest since most of the class was comprised of women. The prisoners were primarily African-American or Spanish-American males.

The woman who walked in front of me was the daughter of the NYS Commissioner of the prison system. She was a blond Viking who towered over my 5'7" frame. As we were walking between the two rows of prisoners, I heard a voice say,

"Hey, Babe, Do you want a date?"

I thought that the prisoner was talking to the Valkyrie in front of me, so I didn't glance around, but when I heard the question again, I focused on a prisoner who was sitting on the floor of his cell. He was still behind bars.

I nervously quickened my pace; I wasn't interested in starting a conversation.

At the end of our tour, five prisoners volunteered to be interviewed. Our professor thought it would prove to be a learning experience for everyone who was involved.

I was selected to be part of the group that met with the prisoners. I knew that my professor respected my extensive teaching experience and my maturity. Of course, the professor was also part of the group.

The prisoners thought the meeting was a lark. I believe that they wanted to impress us with their control of the cell block. They smoked in front of us while a prisoner acted as a lookout.

One question we asked each man was what crime had they committed. They all proudly admitted to being either a murderer or a rapist. The murderers were "lifers" who were incarcerated for the remainder of their lives.

I also had my first viewing of a "fish". A young, blond man was the plaything for a group of Spanish men. His blond hair, slight frame and slumped posture marked him as a victim amidst the group of buffed, dark men. He was dressed in a white shirt and pants while his entourage was dressed in prison clothing. His bearing, posture and clothing presented a clear picture of what role he played within the group.

Chapter 56

"My name is Maria A. Beurmann"

The Niskayuna teacher, who introduced me to hiking in the Adirondacks, also gave me the opportunity to sail on a 27 foot boat to Newfoundland. The crew consisted of my friend, her husband - who acted as the captain of the boat - their daughter and Ellen, the NYC friend who had accompanied my daughter and me on my second cross-country trip.

I lacked the qualities to be a good sailor. I got seasick crossing the strait from Nova Scotia to Newfoundland and could not move from my bunk without losing total control of my digestive system. My friend's daughter and I stayed below for a day and night while my friend cooked and staunchly withstood the smell of the cooking gas and the pitching roll of the sailboat.

The huge grey swells that I could view through the porthole, when I had the energy to raise my head, made my gorge rise. Thankfully, my friend and her husband were able to withstand the mercurial winds, the piercing cold and the need to steer the boat and trim the sails. The fifth passenger, the city dweller, enjoyed the seascape and was well enough to obey the "captain's" directives when the boat was in full sail or ready to anchor.

The couple who owned the boat had made this trip countless times and they enjoyed bringing different groups of friends on their escapades. On this trip, we were to complete one of their favorite sails. We were to tour the southern coast of Newfoundland, climb some of the 1,000 foot bluffs and visit rustic villages for fish and conversation.

The southern coast is rugged, primitive and empty except for small villages that cling tenaciously to the rocky shores. There are few roads and many empty buildings in the shrub-filled interior. If a family desired a summer place, all it needed to do was travel a short distance and take residence in one of the empty dwellings. Much of their interiors had been ransacked and stripped by visitors who used the material for firewood or as furnishings for their primary homes.

When we were in Newfoundland, we discovered that the inhabitants were paid to bear children. It was common for the children, when they matured, to leave home and their families to find a better life in the more populated areas, or in another locality.

The southern coast is also isolated. Caribou frequent the open areas and a traveler is inundated with clouds of aggressive blackflies. A head net is a necessity to avoid getting eaten alive.

On our tour, we stopped at a village of about 20 homes that, incongruously, had a landing pad for a doctor or medical personnel. The doctor or dentist would annually visit the village in a helicopter to deal with medical problems.

The village was primitive and polluted. The waters around the shoreline were littered with garbage. Moldering fish joined used diapers and offal. We went into a store to buy produce, but only fish, wrinkled and dried-out vegetables and candy were on display. The lack of healthy food might have accounted for the villagers' blackened, stubby teeth.

Only the village men came to speak with us, but they focused their attention on our captain and studiously ignored the women and the little girl. My friend's husband joked that the villagers thought that the women on board were his wives. We did not have a chance to speak with any village women for they locked themselves in their homes and peered at us from parted curtains.

The few women who watched us from their stoops looked twice their age. They wore dark clothes and were overweight. Their children, who scampered on the rocky pathways, likewise displayed black stubs for teeth when they laughed. They were more comfortable commenting on the boat and the crew than were the village women.

My friend's daughter and I had meshed from the beginning of our trip. Since she and I had little to do with sailing the boat, we talked. I regaled her with tales of Loki and Odin and eventually expanded to the Greek and Roman gods and goddesses. She loved the stories and would beg for more as we sailed from village to village.

When we stopped at a village to buy fish, the little girl and I would sit in the sun encased in warm clothing and we would watch the fishermen unload their daily catches of bugged-eyed, red-skinned fish. The fishermen would slit the fish, throw the innards in the surrounding waters and offer the cleaned fish to my friend's husband.

My friend would make the most surprising and tasty dishes for breakfast, lunch and dinner. One of my favorite dishes that she cooked on dank days was a hearty cheese soup. She had to have had a strong constitution to cook in a pitching boat that stank of cooking gas.

When we anchored the boat in the fjords, we completed some difficult climbs up the 1,000 ft. bluffs. There were no paths. We bush-wacked up the bluff and had to scramble from one precarious boulder to another. My friend and I would hold the little girl's hands as we ascended the bluffs. The youngster was not happy and would often cry as the blackflies bit her arms and swarmed about her head net.

The large, moss-covered boulders, that littered the bluff, reminded me of huge marbles that had been tossed haphazardly by a giant's hand, so when crossing from one boulder to another, yawning gaps could be seen between and below the boulders.

I had empathy for the little girl, for her crying did not abate. It was unpleasant to constantly swat at the clouds of black flies. We all wore head nets and we had sprayed our arms and clothes with bug repellent, but the Newfoundland variety of black flies were made of sterner stuff. They did not give up gorging themselves on our blood until night descended and we were ensconced in the boat.

It felt like we were midgets in a giant's play land. The area was wild, empty and lonesome. If we looked down from the top of the bluffs we could see our 27 foot boat in the fjord looking like a toy in a bathtub.

When we reached the top of the bluff, I took the time to bathe, for there was a large pond of invitingly clear, cool water that reached up to my knees. Surprisingly, I was not bothered at the top of the bluff by the ubiquitous black flies. On one of our sailing excursions along the southern coast, we sailed into Devil's Gorge. It resembled a fjord - a long narrow inlet with steep cliffs caused by glacial erosion - much like Norway's topography. We anchored there for the night.

Around midnight, while the rest of the crew slept in the confines of the cabin, I dressed in winter gear (even though it was July) and listened to the keening wind and watched the spectacular and eerie lightshow in the sky.

Devil's Gorge
(Newfoundland)

Winds sweep the gorge.
Invade the secluded inlet
Imprisoned by barren cliffs.

Numbing midnight cold.

Mainsail shudders,
Metal clangs,
Company for a solitary soul.

White light slashes starry skies.

Aurora Borealis
Stuns the observer,
A dust mote in God's eye.

When the week ended, Ellen and I made reservations to ride on the ship, "The Blue Nose" that would bring us back to Nova Scotia. My friends continued to sail around the southern coast of Newfoundland.

Chapter 57

"My name is Maria A. Beurmann"

While Ellen and I were crossing the strait from
Newfoundland to Nova Scotia, the earth moved for me for
the second time.

We had parked ourselves in lounge chairs on the large
ship so to avoid becoming seasick during the voyage. In the
middle of the crossing, three men pulled up chairs near us so
that they could engage us in conversation. They introduced
themselves.

One was a "Newfie," or a native of Newfoundland,
who was traveling on his own. The other two men were Jim,
a man in his late 30's, and his oldest friend. Both were on
vacation and had been biking on their Harley-Davidsons in

Nova Scotia and Newfoundland. They were on their return voyage to their home in Michigan.

The Newfie immediately tried to engage me in a conversation. He was pleasant, but was very assertive and kept crowding my space as he sat on the deck in front of my chair. I was not interested in him, but was intrigued by the 30-year-old man who was closer to my age. Both he and his older friend worked as engineers for the Honeywell Company in Michigan.

Jim had an immediate impact on me. I felt light-headed when I gazed at him. My mouth went dry, my head pounded and I could sense the blood coursing through my veins. As my Uncle Joe would say, "I was hit by the Italian thunderbolt."

Finally, when the man from Newfoundland realized that I was not interested in him, he shifted his attention to Ellen. I had spent the afternoon hours listening to the group, but had not added much to the conversation since I was spellbound by Jim.

He had watched the Newfie's interactions with me and had noticed my reticence in joining the general conversation. He had to have noticed that I was fixated on him during the remainder of the trip. Since I had not received any direct response from him, I believed that he was not interested in me, so I left my chair to walk around the moving ship.

As I stood against the railing wondering why I had such a response to this stranger, I felt his presence next to me. He did not say anything, and we both watched the prow of the ship slice into the foaming water.

He spoke quietly and asked where Ellen and I were staying once we reached Nova Scotia's shoreline. He added that he and his friend were heading for an Irish pub once we landed. He asked me to join him at the pub for supper and an evening of Irish entertainment.

Conveniently, there was a campground near the landing site. Ellen and I found a camping spot where we erected the Eureka tent and laid out our sleeping bags. We changed our clothes so to better accommodate an evening at an Irish pub.

When we arrived at the pub, the Irish shanties and ballads were in full swing and the patrons were joining in the choruses. Jim and his friend were already there. I sat next to Jim and we immediately held hands under the table. I placed my palm on his leg and without a word moved closer to him. I swear that I felt the electricity between us. It was a visceral communication, since we didn't feel a need to exchange a word. All I could do was gaze at him.

As the hours passed, Ellen began to fidget. She was uncomfortable with our silence and to break the tension she said that she needed sleep since we were heading for Rexford, New York the next morning. I was disappointed to leave Jim, but to assuage Ellen we left the two men at the pub and retired to our tent.

I was anxious because of the day's events and could not sleep. Nothing seemed to bother Ellen because she immediately fell asleep. Several hours passed as I stared at the tent's shadowed ceiling and listened to the nocturnal chorus of crickets and cicadas. I was not surprised to hear the sound of a cruising motorcycle as it slowly passed our tent.

I quickly put on my clothes, but by the time I exited the tent and stood on the dirt road, the motorcycle had left the campgrounds. Jim and I had not spoken at the pub of getting together at the campsite, but I knew that the lone rider had been Jim. I was intensely disappointed that I had missed being with him. I returned to my tent and lay awake for most of the night.

As Ellen and I were heading home, I mentioned to her that I had extended an invitation to Jim to come to visit me on his way home to Michigan. Ellen scoffed and told me that I was dreaming if I expected a man, whom we had just met, to go hundreds of miles out of his way to be with a stranger. I, however, had felt the electricity between us and I hoped to see him.

We arrived safely at my home and began to unpack. The phone rang in the early evening hours and I sensed that it was Jim. He had arrived in Clifton Park and was heading for my house. I offered him and his friend lodging for the evening and dinner if he had not already eaten.

Jim took a shower. I stood by my bedroom window gazing outside as the moon slowly rose over the tree tops. When finished with his preparations, Jim stood behind me, embraced me and quietly watched the trees stir in the moonlight. Again, we spoke little during the entire evening, but it was a magical time for me; one that I will remember for years to come.

In the morning, I fixed breakfast for all my guests. Jim and I made our farewells as his friend packed his pannier packs. We exchanged a chaste kiss and no promises were made. I waved a farewell as both men rode off on their motorcycles. The memory of this unusual but romantic tryst still brings me comfort, for it was an once-in-a-lifetime experience that surely would never occur again.

Chapter 58

"My name is Maria A. Beurmann"

My daughter was back in school, my mother was settled in an adult home, I was finished with my Master's degree in Criminal Justice and I needed a job in this new field. My wish was to gain a position that would incorporate the new knowledge of the criminal justice system with the skills that I acquired through teaching.

I had checked with a headhunter as to the availability of jobs for former teachers. He was not optimistic about my chances. He believed that teachers are not capable of doing anything but teach. He warned me that I would encounter problems fitting in the business arena.

The professor, whom I now considered a friend, promised to be on the lookout for a job which would combine my new degree and my past teaching experiences. This was the law professor who organized our visits to the NYS prisons. He soon called to inform me of a two-year grant position with the New York State Division for Youth in Albany, N.Y. I set up an interview with the Director of that unit.

The grant work was to analyze the efficacy of educational programs that existed in New York State's juvenile prisons. New York City would not be included in the survey since its educational system was not well organized and was not considered effective.

I arrived for my interview and was introduced to the director. He took one look at me and exclaimed in front of his employees,

"You asked me to take off my belt. My pants nearly fell off."

I was a bit embarrassed, especially to be the center of attention, but I did recall meeting him at Albany's International Airport a couple of days before the interview.

In between my "real" jobs, I worked for a temp agency so that I could earn money to pay my bills. While I was waiting for a more lucrative job to materialize, I held the position of Security Supervisor at Albany's airport. My martial arts training, my teaching background and my Master's degree in Criminal Justice had smoothed my way into this position.

As the supervisor, I had asked a man, who turned out to be my future employer, to remove his belt, since the gate kept chiming whenever he passed under it. My brusque request made an impression on him, since he was used to people's respectful demeanor due to his exalted position within the NYS Division for Youth. I had been as professional with him as I would have been with any other potential passenger.

He hired me immediately for a special grant project. For over a year, a young woman and I worked closely together. She had expertise in computer programming and I had many years of experience with educational systems, reading programs and dealing with diverse groups of people. We made a good fit.

We spent months compiling surveys that were geared to specific minors who were, at this time, incarcerated in an institution until a trial occurred and a judge passed sentence on the youngsters' crimes. While these individuals were in holding, they were required to be enrolled in an educational program. I was to judge the outcomes of the educational programs and their effectiveness through a survey.

I contacted the directors of each of the NYS facilities, of which there were over 40, and set a date to individually meet with their classroom teachers to complete the surveys. The instructors were required by law to have each student enrolled in a valid educational program. The assessments specifically requested an analysis of the student's learning problems and information on his or her reading program, progress, attendance and behavior.

Depending on the number of students in each facility, the teacher and I might take one day or the entire weekend to complete the lengthy questionnaires.

I traveled as far north as Lake Superior and visited cities, such as Buffalo, New York, assessing programs. As expected, some of the meetings lasted entire weekends. When the students were few, the inquiries only took several hours to complete.

Once I had visited all the sites, my partner and I inserted the coded information from the surveys into the computer and a final tome was created that was submitted for review to the NYS Legislative body. The law-making body would then determine if the educational programs were to continue in each facility or if changes needed to be made.

The majority of the detention facilities greeted me with enthusiasm, since I was the first state person who had an actual teaching background, and because I brought a large box of doughnuts as a motivator. Normally, if a representative of NYS Education Department met with them, that person had little or no classroom experience.

At one institution, the director was unusually helpful. He may have wished to provide me with a more in-depth look of his facility, or he may have wanted to play a joke on me. He selected one of the teenage residents to act as my tour guide. The young man was informative, very cordial and attentive as we walked throughout the buildings. When I praised the young man in front of the director, the man smiled. I later asked him what crime the young man had committed and the director answered,

"He killed his mother."

It calls to mind the axiom "One really cannot judge a book by its cover."

Our grant project proved successful in all but two facilities. When I traveled to Buffalo, New York, where I would have had to remain the entire weekend because of the large number of students enrolled in its educational program, the teacher, in order to avoid our meeting, had taken all his students on a field trip to the city park. I was never able to meet the teacher or complete the questionnaires, but my partner and I informed our employer of the situation. We noted in our report that the teacher's individualized, educational programs did not exist. We had a similar result with another urban site.

All in all, my partner proved to be extremely accomplished and I enjoyed traveling throughout New York State and meeting teachers who did their best under arduous and demanding conditions.

Chapter 59

"My name is Maria A. Beurmann"

When my daughter moved away to attend college, I planned my final extended trip through the Adirondack Preserve. My friend, Ellen, had enjoyed the trip to Newfoundland so much that she jumped at the chance to hike the 133-mile, low-land Northville-Lake Placid (NPT) trail. The strenuous wilderness hike begins at Northville, New York and ends at Lake Placid, New York.

The first two-thirds of the trail is a gradual ascent to a plateau which follows streams and lakes, such as the extensive Long Lake. The other third of the NPT is a valley route between several peaks that had no trails.

The NPT is not for beginners. Hikers need to be experienced because of the trail's length, its ruggedness and potential pitfalls, such as blood blisters, bears, areas inundated by beaver activity and streams that have to be navigated. It was a new experience for Ellen to complete such a rugged hike, and I had some concerns because of her urban background, but she believed she was capable of completing the trip, so we geared up.

We both wanted to earn the blue on white patch from the Schenectady Chapter of the Adirondack Mountain Club that showed that we succeeded in completing the NPT. It didn't matter whether we were going to hike the entire trail at one time or hike it in sections to earn the patch.

We decided to do the trail all at once. We would carry between us any food and equipment that was needed for the entire trip rather than mailing packages of food and equipment to various postal offices in the towns that bordered the trail. The latter was the more common procedure for most hikers of the trail because it lessened the burden of carrying extra weight. We decided to carry all the food and equipment for 14 days, but we hoped to complete the trail from Northville to Lake Placid in less time.

To cut back on weight we carried freeze-dried food, dried fruit, nuts, peanut butter, cheese spreads and depended on a top-of-the-line water filter, so that we could use the streams that we crossed as a source. By the time we had gathered our supplies, we each carried about 35 pounds.

When I first began hiking in the Adirondack Preserve, I was able to drink from the streams without having to use iodine pills or boil the water. Fortunately or unfortunately, depending on your audience, people have infected our water sources in natural areas by urinating or defecating in the streams. Hikers were also prone to washing dishes and themselves with various cleansing products.

Because of people's mistakes, their germs were transferred to a new host, the beaver. The beaver, in turn, expelled its contaminated wastes back into the water. The cycle continued when people took water from the stream to drink or to wash dishes. Regretfully, the beaver is blamed for this new illness, for its common name is "Beaver Fever." The formal name for this disease is Giardia.

Giardia is a parasitic infection of the small intestine. It causes tiredness, stomach cramps, bloating and excessive gas. It begins one to three weeks after exposure and it is quite unpleasant. Thankfully, neither of us was infected during our extensive hike.

Chapter 60

"My name is Maria A. Beurmann"

It rained most of the time on the trail, but when we lucked out with a sunny day, we spread out tent and sleeping bags on bushes to dry and air out. We also needed these sunny and hot days to wash our hair and clothes and to tend to our feet, because the constant pressure of hiking over root systems and rough terrain caused blisters and rent toenails.

There were not many hikers completing the NPT that summer. We did see people staying at lean-tos that were close to a road, but they were there to party, so they came prepared with beer and food to celebrate and to camp overnight. To avoid these groups, Ellen and I made it a point to hike long stretches per day and to camp in lean-tos that were more inaccessible. We were not worried about finding open lean-tos for it was a practice, while completing the NPT, to share a lean-to with other hikers if sleeping or cooking space were needed.

We were concerned about the wild life. Thankfully, all we saw of wild animals were bears' slash marks on trees or steaming animal scat on the trail. It did not take us long to discover that the key predator on the trail was man. The wilderness, in reality, is a lawless land. We did not see a single forest ranger during our entire trip, so we were on our own if we were threatened by humans.

We did not wish to be viewed as victims, so we made certain to engage any hiker we encountered in conversation about the trip, other hikers and our own personal experiences on the trail. It felt like the Pony Express, for we exchanged stories, such as the mother and daughter team who were pinned in their tent by a fallen tree. The daughter extricated herself from the tent and swam across a nearby lake to get help at the park ranger station. We were later told by other hikers, whom we passed, that the mother and daughter survived their grueling ordeal.

Most hikers we met were friendly and well prepared, but we crossed paths with some inexperienced hikers. One of these hikers and his dog had to be carted off the trail by an emergency crew, because the young man developed blood blisters on the soles of both feet. He could not put any pressure on his feet and, therefore, could not walk or stand on his own. His friends could not carry him to an exit point, so one of his companions had to run the trail to seek help. His dog was also in bad shape with torn foot pads. It, likewise, had to be ferried off the trail and hospitalized until both the owner and the dog healed.

I made a major mistake before starting the hike. I bought new boots. They were quality hiking boots, but I did not take the time to break them in. Usually, it takes several weeks to break in new boots. Unfortunately, they broke me in. It took six months after the trip to get my toenails to remain on my toes. After 133 miles of trekking through the rugged terrain, my toenails turned black and then fell off. They grew back in, then blackened and fell off again. I was fortunate to have not suffered any long-term injuries; my feet just looked unsightly.

As you may have noticed, I tend to enjoy and recall humorous events and, of course, by traversing 133 miles a funny incident had to occur.

The trip was arduous and toward the end of each day we were exhausted and, subsequently, we became surly. Ellen was the lead on the trail that continued on a bridge that crossed a knee-high stream. I had suggested that we camp at a lean-to on the other side of the bridge. To avoid contaminating the stream, we would have needed to either sleep in the lean-to or set up our tent about 100 feet from the streambed. She was not happy with my suggestion and showed her displeasure by stopping on the bridge. I was tired and did not wish to get into a confrontation with her, so I crossed the bridge to the lean–to where I deposited my heavy backpack.

Instead of bringing her pack to the lean-to, Ellen dropped everything on the bridge and informed me that she was going to take a bath in the stream.

We were in wilderness. There was no one at the lean-to, but being exposed in a shallow stream was not my idea of privacy. I tried to dissuade her from going naked near the open bridge, but she bristled at my suggestion and waded into the slow-moving water.

As I was setting up my sleeping gear in the lean-to, I heard young voices on the trail that we had just covered. The youngsters had to be completing the trail the same way we were – from Northville north to Lake Placid. Suddenly, a small group of boys in full Boy Scout uniforms clambered on the bridge. There was total silence as they stood gaping at Ellen who was kneeling naked in the shallows of the stream. She was ineffectively trying to cover her body with her hands and the arrowroot that grew in the low waters. The boys' high voices mingled with their laughter.

I smothered my amusement at Ellen's plight and did not dare broach the boys' reactions or comments. Since the troop soon moved on to reach a more distant lean-to, Ellen did not have to deal with a reminder of the spectacle she had provided.

After 11 days, we reached the extensive wooden plank walkway that led to the town of Lake Placid. We had subsisted on freeze-dried food, peanut butter and crackers and dried fruit and nuts for most of the trip. A couple of hikers had once willingly shared some of their fresh fruit with us, but it was not enough to satisfy our hunger. We were famished for fresh vegetables, fresh fruit and fruit juices, and pastries. It was still morning when we hit the town, so we headed for a bakery and immediately bought and ate a dozen doughnuts. It took us an entire day of eating to feel satisfied. The steak, baked potatoes, vegetables and the apple pie that we ordered for supper were the most delectable foods that we had experienced in quite a while.

The average time that most hikers take to complete the entire Northville-Lake Placid trail is about 19 days. There are a few who have completed the trail in several days, but they ran the trail with very little food and equipment. Since we wanted to have the total experience, we finished our trip in 11 days without encountering any major injuries or unique species.

Both Ellen and I took great pride in that once-in-a-life accomplishment and we proudly sewed the blue and white NPT patch on our daypacks.

Chapter 61

"My name is Maria A. Beurmann"

After graduating from college, Julia met a man in the Glens Falls area whom she dated for a period of time. Eventually, he asked her to marry him. She agreed to since he was tall, handsome and personable. He was well liked and well known in his town. I believe Julia was also intrigued with his large family, for my family consisted of only two people – my daughter and me.

My daughter and her new husband looked like the perfect couple as they took their wedding vows. The ceremony was well attended and the only complication was the yelling match between his estranged parents. Jay generously paid for the main meal for 200 guests, but a good half of the guests who attended were his family. It was an enjoyable event.

Julia and her husband honeymooned in Italy where my daughter, without any prompting from me, traced records for my parents and her heritage.

Unfortunately, during major conflicts such as World War II, people tended to be rousted from their homes. If their families or homes were destroyed, they often moved to safer localities. Records were not kept and were frequently lost. Julia did not discover any information on my mother, but she did find material on my father.

My father had recorded that he took care of me until I was adopted, as an eight-year-old child, by an American woman. The report was a positive narration of his attentiveness and care; however, none of it was true. I actually had lived with my mother until I was four and was then placed in an orphanage until I was eight. His misplaced recollections may have been his justification for giving up his family, or running away during a time of great stress.

My daughter called me during her honeymoon to tell me of her quest and she asked if I wished her to continue her search for my parents. Because of my experience with my adopted mother's relatives and their greed, I told Julia that I was not interested in knowing more.

The years passed, and Julia bore a boy and a girl; gifts that I prayed for and cherish to this day. The marriage did not thrive, for both adults were from two disparate backgrounds. Soon, my daughter was raising her children on her own. It was a difficult period, because the relationship between the two divorced parents was strained and contentious.

It was not surprising that the marriage did not work. Julia's husband was used to a traditional, male-dominated household where the wife was subservient to the husband. He was used to getting his way. He typifies "a man's man."

Between the two adults, there was a disparity of occupations, goals, interests and personalities. They constantly fought over anything and everything. He enjoyed his extended family and was not happy to spend any holidays away from his parents, brothers or his sports.

He developed a pattern of behavior when Julia brought him to my home to celebrate holiday events. I could have written and followed a script for any special occasion at my home.

I would spend the day preparing a holiday meal. My daughter and her husband would arrive at my home. The television would be immediately tuned to a sports' station. My son-in-law would select a topic and would ambush my daughter with his interpretation of that topic. His wrath would flare to an abnormal degree when she tried to defuse his rage or if she disagreed with him.

Dinner would be served and quickly ingested. Julia would wash the dishes, but would often be distracted by her husband's looming presence.

The quarrel would continue as they moved into the living room. He would be focused on the results of the game on the television. After an hour or two, both adults would collect their gear and leave to drive to his family's celebration which usually lasted the entire evening. I would rush to the bathroom when they left and vomit up my meal.

I began to hate their occasional holiday visits for I knew the script and the ending of the play. Unfortunately, their lives had to follow his plan and my daughter continued to be oppressed and unhappy.

Julia remained silent about the state of her marriage. She has always been private and tends to only confide to her closest friends. I sensed her relationship with her husband was tainted, but I felt powerless to help her, especially when my grandchildren were present. I hoped that a time would arrive where she would gather her resources and take the step to live life on her own terms.

Chapter 62

"My name is Maria A. Beurmann"

Julia has worked for the same company for many years. It is a demanding job, but she still found time and energy, while raising my grandchildren, to earn a Master's degree in Business Administration. She not only holds an important position in a male-dominated business, but she also is keenly involved in fitness programs. She is a life coach and represents and manages diverse training programs. She has presented and developed training seminars throughout the state and has acquired a reputation as a health coach and an anti-aging expert. Her goal is to advise women and men on foods and lifestyle habits that produce healthier lives.

Julia, at one time, intimated that she was lonely. She had had various relationships, but unlike me, could not see herself without a companion. She met her current husband who has brought stability and love into her life.

My new son-in-law is a healthier choice for her. They share more commonalities; the most significant is humor. He is comfortable dealing with my grandchildren and they respect him.

Both work out together and both are writing books that analyze their past lives. They have established new goals and have set new horizons.

The most important aspects of their new lives are that they make each other happy. They also are able to communicate with each other to solve problems.

Chapter 63

"My name is Maria A. Beurmann"

I had been diagnosed with a brain tumor before Julia's second wedding ceremony. The ceremony was, for me, a medicated blur. My brain surgeon had prescribed a steroid to help me heal after I had a biopsy, but my body reacted to the strong medication. I was sick and vertiginous during the wedding ceremony. It also did not help to have to deal with Jay's wife's shenanigans during the reception.

When Jay's wife made her move to disrupt my daughter's reception, I was amazed to note that Jay did nothing to stop his wife's machinations.

Jay is intelligent – he is an engineer – and because of his intelligence I would have thought that he might have protested and made a better choice, especially since it was his daughter's wedding celebration.

My daughter had staged a reception that was suited for children and adults. The food was ordered to appeal to both groups, but the Lake George wedding facility did not allow alcoholic beverages to be served on its premises, since it was a Christian resort.

Jay's wife did not appreciate that regulation. Both the husband and wife enjoy drinking wine, so at the beginning of the late-afternoon reception, she took her entire family and traveled to a northern, Adirondack town to drink. The adults and children returned to the resort around midnight. The adults were high on alcohol and the children were high on adrenaline. Since I was housed on the same floor as my ex-husband's family, I was privy to the partying and the children's antics throughout the night. No one on my floor slept the evening of my daughter's second wedding.

Julia was affected by the wife's lack of sense and her father's betrayal, but my daughter handled the situation with aplomb.

Let me be frank. To this day, I consider Jay's wife's decision to disregard the sanctity of my daughter's wedding a true reflection of her lack of intelligence and class.

My ex-husband's role in her decision puzzled me. I could not understand why he chose drinking over celebrating his daughter's wedding.

Unfortunately, there is a greater rift between my ex-husband and his daughter because of his decision to join his wife's exodus from the wedding.

Chapter 64

"My name is Maria A. Beurmann"

As my daughter achieved a sterling reputation as a director of her company and as she developed her avocations, my grandchildren matured into teenagers. I moved on to enjoy various occupational experiences.

Because of my past position as a Scientific Researcher – my stint with NYS Division for Youth – where I assisted in analyzing educational programs in prisons for delinquent youths – I garnered, through another grant, a position with Albany BOCES. BOCES had been subcontracted by the NYS Education Department to organize a three-day, state-wide Chapter I conference in Albany, N.Y. On this occasion, I was part of a five-person crew.

Each individual on the team had been hired for his or her specific expertise. My task was to create the program for the conference and to manage all the speakers. I published a polished program and then worked closely with the hotel's staff to ascertain that the facility had the necessary equipment and amenities to make the speakers' stay and presentations a success. The conference achieved its goals.

Another position that I held with Albany's BOCES was piloting a California Reading program to NYC teachers. My task was to visit an educational facility in the city for two days per month for five months. I was to initially present the program's objectives, teach the skills to the teachers and then assess the results. The fifty teachers, who represented the various boroughs of NYC, were to apply these new techniques for a month within their classrooms until I returned to teach the next skill set.

Unfortunately, there was a cadre of teachers who blatantly informed me on the first day that they believed that the program that I espoused was a punitive measure forced on them by their school districts. They refused to complete the required work, but did wish to attend the sessions, so I asked them to sit in one section of the meeting room and try not to interfere with the learning experience. Once they realized that I was not going to press the issue, they spent the instructional hours during the five months we met knitting, quietly speaking among themselves, or drinking coffee while I trained the remaining teachers.

I had never had to deal with NYC's educational system, but it is quite different from the regulations set for the remainder of the state by NYS Education Department. A teacher from the group, who was my guide, admitted that the city's educational system was usually left to fend for itself, because its dysfunctional elements could not be managed or controlled by Albany.

Chapter 65

"My name is Maria A. Beurmann"

When the grant funded projects were completed, I obtained a managerial position with the nationally known Sylvan Learning Centers. The owner was especially impressed with the two books that I had published on the poetry and photography of the Adirondack Mountains, but my teaching experience was the essential element that procured me my position.

I held the title of Regional Coordinator for both the Clifton Park and Albany facilities. For six years, my tasks were to hire and train teachers, pilot new educational programs and order educational materials. I also taught students, managed their programs, visited their schools and periodically met with their parents. The parents spent an inordinate amount of money, sometimes even their pension checks, to provide their children with programs that focused on math, study skills, writing or reading techniques.

The programs that had been developed for Sylvan Learning Centers reminded me of the curriculums that I had coordinated for my students at Niskayuna High School. I believed that these educational programs were comprehensive and allowed the students to grow and succeed in whatever options they chose.

During the summer when my mother was taking her last breaths, I piloted for Sylvan Learning Center at Union College, a John Hopkins' writing program. It was a program designed and aimed at gifted students in the tri-city area. It integrated various activities that would motivate students to create unique essays and writing assignments.

After six years, the owner of the Sylvan Learning Center modified her goals – she wanted an invitation to join the Millionaire's Circle at the annual meeting. In order to be invited, a center was required to earn a set amount of money. The managers; therefore, were forced to convince parents to enroll their children in more programs.

Our jobs became more demanding, especially when we visited local schools to speak of our programs. This was not effective, since schools believed that by our existence we were inadvertently suggesting that the schools were not doing their job. We created more dissention by visiting the students' teachers.

The owner also wished to revamp the staff. Her belief was that the leadership needed to be younger, so to accommodate this new vision, she hired a young director, then brought in her best friend and finally selected her son and daughter to lead both facilities.

I had sensed the drastic changes that were going to occur, so I left. The owner had been going through menopause, so the job was extremely stressful for everyone employed there. The only recourse, that was available to us to negate the stress of the job, was to meet at a local drinking hole during the week. We spent hours venting about the owner's mood swings and the week's problems. When I left the center, two other managers also decided to search for new jobs.

Ironically, the young director did not work out. She spent her time on the computer e-mailing her friends and creating pornographic cards. She was inexperienced, was quite impressed with her title, but had a poor work ethic. She was fired. It was a tumultuous year for everyone.

Chapter 66

"My name is Maria A. Beurmann"

I immediately contacted Pearson's National Evaluation Systems in Malta, New York. Pearson is managed by the NYS Education Department, which in turn determines the guidelines for a teacher's accreditation. Pearson trains retired and active teachers to holistically score all of NYS's teachers' certification tests for any new teacher who is going to teach in any field, such as math, science, shop or languages. Because of its thorough work at scoring tests and training teachers, other states, such as Arizona and Illinois, defer to Pearson to score their teachers' certification tests.

The training to score the tests takes an entire morning. Each essay or test could range from one to three pages. It is difficult to cheat, for candidates do not know what topic had been selected for them that test day. Topics can range from class management, motivation and disciplinary techniques to parental and community contacts. When I first began working for Pearson, the candidates wrote their responses by hand, but within the last five years the responses have been computerized.

After the training sessions, two or three days are set aside for scoring the essays. The scorers laboriously read the essays and then give the essays a holistic grade that can range from 1 to 4. The majority of the candidates pass, but some fail. They would have to reapply to retake the exams. At the end of each scoring day, our eyes were bloodshot and our backs were cramped and stiff.

The worst responses were from New York City. We never knew the gender, nationality or race of the candidate, but on occasions, the respondents would include details of the school or city in which they worked. As we read the responses from NYC, we were distressed by the quality of the writing and examples of unrealistic teaching techniques.

My final paying position as an accredited teacher was as a tutor for home-bound students in Scotia Middle and High Schools. It had been a while - since my time with the

Albany School District- that I had seen such abject poverty and unusual family dynamics.

The nine years that I worked part-time for this school system was an experience. I thoroughly enjoyed working with the staff and, especially with the vice-principal of the high school. He went out of his way to accommodate my needs with the students who often were the most difficult to work with.

Some of the tutoring assignments made a lasting impression. When one of my student's parents moved to Scotia, she discovered that she could manipulate the school and the town government into granting her and her family expensive financial and emotional assistance. While I taught her daughter at their home, various representatives from different agencies, such as social workers, religious representatives, legal aid, etc. would appear and spend an hour speaking with the parent. She would often boast to me that she could get anyone to do what she wanted.

Her boyfriend would hover near my student as the mother's newest addition to the family crawled on a filthy floor. When I first started teaching her daughter, I had overheard the mother telling her daughter not to let me into the kitchen. As I was quite thirsty one day, since I was constantly talking over the mother's conversations with the various agents, I got up and went into the kitchen. Pizza boxes were stacked head-height and I saw fleeting, roach-like shapes scurrying among food-encrusted dishes. Feces from the toddler's diapers were deposited on the floor. That was the last and only time I walked into the kitchen.

The same student would often ridicule my suggestions on how to complete her assignments. Her mother's boyfriend defended me one day and told the teenager that he would take her over his knee and spank her. My student picked up a butcher knife and replied that she would knife him if he touched her. I was appalled by the family dynamics but, of course, as a visitor I could not volunteer my opinion.

I could have refused to tutor that student because the above incident might have been construed as a dangerous situation. Out of all the students that I worked with, I only refused to meet with one family. The boy was physically abusing his mother while I was at their home. To protect the mother from the beatings, I had to constantly step between them. Because the danger might have extended to my person, the school recommended that he be taken out of the home and placed in an institution for troubled youths.

Another student whom I taught, was a ninth grader who already had a two- year old child at home. The student did not believe that she needed to work or complete homework so she chose to fail almost all of her courses.

As I was working with her daughter, the mother would scream at the children in her day-care center. The father would watch pornographic videos that used the "F" word. Two year-old children were being educated by a five-year-old child on the meaning of the middle finger salute and I spent the two hours each day trying to avoid stepping on the toddlers who were sleeping under our work table.

When I insisted that the student needed to complete her schoolwork, the mother contacted the school and told it that she wanted me gone. Her excuse to roust me was that I was prejudiced against students who had babies.

I agreed that it was time to end the program, since the student intentionally placed her instructional texts under a leaking roof, and tended to deliberately lose her materials and her assignments. I have often wondered what has become of the student since education seemed the least of her concerns.

I also had never in my 30 plus years of teaching across NYS come across so many students with anxiety issues. These problems motivated the students and their parents to depend on medications. At times, the medications so affected the students that they chose to remain home. They then became more depressed since they spent the entire day playing games or watching television. The only time they left the comfort of their homes, was to walk or ride a bicycle to the local school to meet their friends after the school day ended.

These were frustrating cases, especially when the student decided not to be home when he or she had class with me. They would use the class time to wander the streets.

Sadly, the students' problems were so complex – poverty, the suicide of a sibling, lack of interest in education, parental neglect, divorce – that I probably affected only a few of my students. Their lives were their reality; school was a mirage that could not change their disastrous situations.

However, because of my organizational skills and teaching techniques, I gained a reputation of being able to handle and teach almost any problem student. I was in constant demand and was once told that the school could use my talents 18 hours a day. Unfortunately, my upcoming brain operation ended my connection with Scotia-Glenville's high school.

Chapter 67

"My name is Maria A. Beurmann"

The final leg of my journey, which will move us into the present, began without fanfare. There was not a hint of the upcoming four-year hiatus. I had been enjoying a carefree life where I wandered throughout our nation or embraced new events.

I was shocked to discover that I had been carrying, for many years, a silent killer in my brain. The subsequent brain surgery was the third trauma to my skull. My scalp is now a roadmap of my life.

I had been working at a computer for several hours. When I went to stand, my left leg and arm went numb and my left eye made a popping noise. I had to wait for five minutes before I felt I could adequately and safely drive home. A martial arts breathing exercise kept me awake while I was driving. When I arrived home, I immediately contacted my neighbors and they drove me to a medical facility.

Tests were conducted and a heart attack and a stroke were ruled out. To make certain that all bases were covered, the hospital administered a CAT scan. It determined that I had a sizeable brain tumor which was identified as a benign, level two, Oligiodendroglioma.

Our medical system seems to have a morbid fascination with a new patient. Within minutes of my CAT scan, three doctors approached me; two of them immediately diagnosed my tumor as cancerous while the third vehemently stated that it was impossible for the first two doctors to determine that I had cancer.

My heart seized, and I felt that I was going to have a heart attack when I heard what the first two doctors had to say. Eventually, I was given medications to reduce my anxiety and to avoid brain seizures.

The third doctor insisted that it is difficult to determine if a patient has cancer if a biopsy and an analysis of the tissue was not completed.

A biopsy was scheduled and completed. I spent one night in the hospital and insisted that I leave the next morning. I had not been able to get a wink of sleep in the ICU between ambulances bringing in new patients, nurses coming in to administer tests and complete blood work and patients groaning in pain.

After that experience, I learned that a person could become increasingly worse if he or she is forced to remain in a medical facility for a longer period of time.

When I asked my surgeon to recommend a qualified brain surgeon, he suggested a reputable surgeon who worked at the Brigham and Women's Hospital in Boston, Massachusetts. He had the expertise to remove my 6.8 mm. brain tumor.

Julia took off from work and braved the heavy traffic to meet with the surgeon. We were both put off by his officious manner.

I'm not certain if he wished to intimidate us, but he pinned all my x-rays with the tumor prominently displayed on the walls of his office. He was very abrupt and arrogant as he spoke to us about the operation.

I *was* intimidated!

He did not discuss any alternative methods. He only offered surgery as an option. He informed us that I would soon get a call from his assistant to set a date for the operation.

Months passed and we did not receive any notification of the date for surgery. Julia e-mailed the PA and the responses were terse, but not informative. No date was scheduled.

Chapter 68

"My name is Maria A. Beurmann"

I finally received a call from my insurance company. The request for surgery in Boston was rejected because there were two surgeons in the Albany Medical Hospital who had expertise in the specialized operation that I required.

More weeks passed with no word from Boston. Finally, the PA called with a date for the operation. I told him we were no longer interested in Boston because the surgery had been denied by my insurance company. I told him that the operation was going to take place in Albany.

My daughter and I had waited for over five months to receive word from the Boston hospital, but when I spoke to their representative about the change in plans, and that they were losing me as a patient, I received, in one day, five calls from the Boston Hospital. One caller requested that I still travel to Boston to have the surgery. Another suggested that I ignore my insurance's decision. I asked the representative who exactly was to pay for the operation. That person chose not to respond to my facetious retort.

After the fifth call, I told the representative that he had better have a conversation with the PA because the doctor's assistant had screwed up.

Once I met with the surgeon at Albany's Medical Hospital, he allowed me some leeway with my schedule. From the time I learned of my tumor, I was hesitant and terrorized to undergo the surgery, because I had been informed that the operation might affect my hearing, vision, my mobility and my vocalization, or it might kill me.

The doctor understood my concerns, but after several visits and MRI's he strongly stated that if I procrastinated any longer he might not be able to operate; the tumor had begun to send tendril to the remainder or the brain. He also showed me on the X-ray how it had been steadily growing during the past months. His serious demeanor led me to schedule a date for the operation, but I needed to first attend my daughter's second marriage. When the celebrations were over, I set the date for my brain surgery.

On November 9, 2016, I underwent a seven-hour-long surgical procedure at the Albany Medical Hospital, and was able to get out of my hospital bed within a day or two. This operation was the culmination of three years of hospital visits, numerous MRI's, medical mistakes and various medications to which I was often allergic. When the surgery was scheduled, I had gotten to the point where I had lost faith in the medical community.

As I lay in the ICU after the brain surgery, I disassociated myself from the chaos in the room and felt myself become extremely calm. It no longer mattered to me that my head had been cut open and that my blood pressure was rising. It was no longer my concern that my ICU nurse was becoming more anxious by the minute. Her attempts to pump me full of drugs to counter the spike no longer interested me.

I welcomed my daughter's hand in mine and that I had her support. I felt that her life was balanced and that she could face the future with hope with her new husband and her two children. There are stories of people dying and seeing white light and a long tunnel when a body's soul or energy bleeds into the cosmos, but I saw no light at the end of a tunnel, and there was no escort in heavenly raiment as I began to lose consciousness.

I wanted to tell Julia that I was leaving her, so I said "I'm dying."

I had accomplished much in my life and was not really interested in undergoing any more medical procedures, nor was I willing to face any more problems.

Julia was incensed by my statement and yelled, "What are you saying?"

The ICU nurse had been on the phone frantically trying to contact my surgeon. She continued to inject me with various medications that were to arrest my dangerously high blood pressure. I heard her say in response to my declaration,

"Not on my watch."

Chapter 69

"My name is Maria A. Beurmann"

When my blood pressure returned to acceptable levels and I was cognizant of my surroundings, Julia lost her temper.

"This is not normal. It is not normal for you to be this anxious."

Months later, while I was undergoing radiation treatments, I contacted my case manager at the CDPHP insurance company. I mentioned my daughter's concerns. Her reply was:

"Did you ever think that you might have PTSD? You have been in a war and have had some unusual things happen to you."

She suggested that, once all the treatments were completed, I should contact a specialist who might help relieve my anxiety levels.

While I was recuperating from the effects of the surgery, I was able to add to my collection of humorous events.

I am psychologically driven to get daily exercise, even if it is only walking a mile. The day after my brain surgery, I felt impelled to walk. I was dressed in the ubiquitous, blue-flowered print that every hospital patient is required to wear. I had tied it at my neck, but didn't bother to tie it at the waist.

I was a mess, since I had not been able to take a shower. My head was sticky with blood and seepage from my wound. I looked a fright, but the urge to move overcame my vanity.

My hospital floor was laid out in a series of squares, so I resolved to walk a square several times. It was very early in the morning, but the hospital was a beehive of activity. There were nurses giving out medications, men completing custodial work and aides serving breakfast.

I was aware that people were curious about my appearance as I moved down the hall past empty carts and beds. I didn't pay any mind to the glances until a young nurse approached me. She put her arm around my shoulders and said,

"Dearie, what are you doing?"

Since it was pretty obvious what I was doing, I looked at her and said,

"I need to walk."

She tightened her hold on my shoulders and sympathetically said, "But you can't walk around like this."

She pointed to the back of my gown.

"And you can't be alone."

Again, I looked at her. First of all, as a 7th degree black belt in karate and with my experiences as a mountaineer, I had never been called "Dearie."

What is wrong with this woman?

She moved behind me and tied the gown together at the waist. My looks didn't really matter to me at this point. After all I had experienced, an exposed backside was the least of my worries, but now the astonished stares made sense.

She had me put on another gown on top of the first gown, but this tied in the front to provide more coverage. She led me gently back to my hospital bed.

I considered other people's sensibilities during the afternoon and made certain I was fully clothed when I asked a nurse to accompany me around another square. I was determined to get as much exercise as possible while I was hospitalized. I wanted and needed to get on with my life, so the more exercise I got the quicker I could leave the building.

Later in the day, to entertain myself, I told the new shift nurse my morning's escapade. She looked at me and said with a smile on her face.

"Ah, you're the one!"

Chapter 70

"My name is Maria A. Beurmann"

Today is the first anniversary of my brain surgery. I have healed more quickly the second time around. The steroid that I took after my biopsy hindered the healing process, because I was allergic to the medication. The key difference between the two recovery periods was the medication.

For those of you who have to undergo any major surgery, if possible, avoid steroids. I had many side effects; vomiting, dizziness and a bloody mouth and throat. Steroids are brutal. I felt constantly ill. I lacked energy, got tired easily and was not interested in eating.

Do the necessary homework and research the least intrusive solutions to your medical problem(s). I was fortunate to have a case manager from my insurance agency – CDPHP- who was able to answer questions, offer suggestions and lessen my anxiety.

Unfortunately, my first surgeon from St. Peter's Hospital did not exhibit the qualities that I expected from a doctor who took a bore sample of my brain. The steroid that he recommended, that was intended to promote healing, actually made me ill. When I sent him a two-page missive asking him for solutions to the problems the steroid caused, he responded by telling me that he did not have the time to answer my questions or address my concerns.

When Julia and I met with him in his office, he was more interested in watching my daughter bend over to pick up her purse than in focusing on my questions. Needless to say, I never visited that doctor again, even though as we were leaving his office, he patted me on the back and said,

"We're still friends, aren't we?"

He was a doctor, I believe, who was more interested in maintaining a pleasant facade than in explaining the results of the surgery, or the benefits of a medication.

The doctor, who did my major brain surgery at Albany Medical Hospital, listened when I told him that I was not interested in taking steroids after the operation. He acquiesced and offered Tylenol for pain and discomfort.

I learned that, in any medical situation, the patient has to be proactive. Mistakes are easy to make when there is a human element involved, so a patient has to be aware and has to become self-educated. I noted several medical mistakes made by doctors and nurses during these past four years and the only way I avoided the negative results of those oversights was to remain hyper-vigilant.

To heal more quickly, I'd advise to exercise every day for a short period of time. The easiest exercise is to walk, but don't over-do it. Naps are also a necessity. An hour or two of rest is refreshing and it allows a person to complete minor tasks in- between. As a songwriter once wrote, "Some days are diamonds; some are coal."

Sometimes, when one is plagued with intermittent sleep, a person can pass the hours re-reading a favorite book, playing a favorite song, watching a favorite movie, or researching authors or musicians on the television or computer. Mix the music with a cup of ginger or peppermint tea. (Ginger is the best solution to nausea or an upset stomach).

Be sure to contact friends and visit local eateries to break the boredom of the day while healing. People are very receptive to a cry for companionship when one is ill or recuperating.

EPILOGUE

The Odyssey of a War Orphan was intended to be cathartic. My life has been a journey that has had its peaks and valleys. It was not my intent to search for clarity through this work; however, I was able to air some issues for myself. I may never resolve others. This memoir allowed me to vent, and it will probably prove to be less expensive than paying an analyst or a psychiatrist.

I have often joked with my friends that I equate myself to a flower. When I arrived in the USA, I was a bud – insular and closed. In my 30's, 40's and 50's, I bloomed; full of color, life and vigor ready and willing to travel, tackle mountains and life's obstacles.

Now, I have a family, have traveled and earned plaudits for my life's work, but I am bruised, wilted and wrinkled and leached of color, but I am still willing to grace any table.

I have lived well, have grasped life whenever possible and have attempted to pay back through teaching young and not so young people; however, as Frank Sinatra has sung,

"I have lived a life that's full, I traveled each and every highway and more, much more, I did it my way."

I have my daughter and my grandchildren to offset my failures. They are making their mark on this world. I bequeath to them the happiness and the lessons I have garnered in my life.

Recommendations for a full life!

. Be true to yourself

. . Take pride in your achievements

. Cherish your family

. Search for honest friends

. Travel - there are so many lessons to be learned in wild places

But, I am not done yet...In my heart, I am still a flower in full bloom.

"I've been lately thinking about my life's time,
All the things I've done and how it's been.

I have to say it;
How it's been a good life after all.

For though life has been good to me
There's so much to do...

I'd like to sail away
And dance across the mountains on the moon."

- John Denver